The Road to MEGA SUCCESS

David,
Wishing you
The Very
Best -
Tom

The Road to MEGA SUCCESS

Simple Strategies for Enriching the Bottom Line

A Strategic Personal and Business Financial Management Guide

LOUIS G. HUTT, JR.
Esq., C.P.A.

JOY Publishers

www.louhutt.com

Disclaimer Statement

This publication contains the opinions and ideas of its author. It is intended to provide helpful and informative material on the subject matter covered. It is sold with the understanding that the author and publisher are not engaged in rendering professional services in the book. If the reader requires personal assistance or advice, a competent professional should be consulted.

The author and publisher specifically disclaim any responsibility for any liability, loss or risk, personal or otherwise, which is incurred as a consequence, directly or indirectly, of the use and application of any of the contents of this book.

For information regarding personal appearances, interviews or purchases please contact the publisher at:

Joy Publishers, an affiliate of The Hutt Co. LLC
10500 Little Patuxent Pkwy
Parkview Building, Suite 640
Columbia, Maryland 21044
www.louhutt.com

Editorial and Development: Mahoganey Hutt-Butler, Esq.
Cover Photo by www.kimberlyportraits.com

Printed in the United States of America at BCP Digital Printing, Inc. • Baltimore, Maryland

ISBN-13 978-0-692-77685-8

To my phenomenal wife, Nellie and
my children Mahoganey, Louis and Eboney
who make me proud to be called Dad.

CONTENTS

ACKNOWLEDGEMENTS

Virtually every important breakthrough toward my adolescence, academic and career advancement has been directly or indirectly attributable, to my wife Nellie, and my parents Joyce and Louis G. Hutt, Sr. They paved the way for me to reach the next level.

My wife's unwavering love, support and companionship has been a source of strength through life's highs and lows. She has been in my corner privately and publicly to encourage, console and advise. Nellie's belief in me and her many personal sacrifices enabled me to pursue my dreams. Even with a demanding professional career of her own as an Appeals Judge she also has been a wonderful and loving mother to our children. Looking back over a lifetime, my wife has certainly been the best thing that ever happened for me.

Despite very humble beginnings, I was also blessed with a mother and father who loved, nurtured and educated me. They would not rest until they had indeed prepared me for life's journey. My mother taught me how to reason and think for myself rather than just go along just to get along with the crowd. She prodded me to assess life's situations and make personal decisions based on simple principles and sound values. She also grilled me on the golden rule to treat other people the way I would want to be treated. On the other hand, my father focused on life long lessons involving personal integrity, responsibility and dependability. Rather than rely on words, he demonstrated these ideals by setting a positive example everyday as a husband, father and doer.

I know without the time, attention and love of my wife, mother and father I would not be where I am today. Very deservedly, I dedicate this book in their honor.

Of all the personal ambitions I have sought to fulfill, composing a book certainly ranks very high on the list. My supportive wife Nellie gave me the green light to embark on this project while we were on a long overdue vacation in the Virgin Islands. However, I seriously doubt at the time she had any idea finishing this work would become my obsession. Her accommodation, patience and support throughout was remarkable.

I was also very fortunate to have a core team of advisors who not only participated in the vetting of ideas and content, but continually reassured me that the end was in site. My law partner and daughter, Mahoganey Hutt Butler, and associate Mary Kay Boler guided my efforts from the beginning to the end of the process. My son Louis G. Hutt, III, also a CPA and business partner challenged my conceptual thinking. He forced me to seek to find the simplest common denominator that would explain financial and business concepts and applications. Likewise, I cherish the constructive feedback I received from my youngest daughter Eboney who is currently a student at Columbia University School of Law. Her legal perspective on business planning was indispensable.

I would not have been in a position to expound on the fundamentals of business and financial management had my college accounting professor, Robert Virgil, PhD not chose to mentor and befriend me. More than simply a teacher, he served as a personal coach. Confirmation from someone in the upper echelon of the accounting profession was not only validation, but spark that sent me on a tear. The momentum boost, lead me to broaden my professional horizon not only in business but the legal profession as well. I successfully passed both the CPA and Bar exams.

To my founding business partners, I also owe much thanks. They helped make possible a rewarding private practice with countless opportunities to grow professionally and to work hand and hand with a wide range of entrepreneurs, business leaders, and tax other professionals. W. Charles Bennett became one of my closet friends in college. Most important, we came to respect each other's academic commitment and work ethic. We graduated and started our careers at Ernst and Young. Eventually, we decided to establish our own firm. We identified a void in the market for management consulting and technical accounting advice for small enterprises, athletes and entertainers.

I have also been blessed to have my younger brother, Kevin T. Hutt, Sr. as a business partner. Kevin was our firm's first full-time employee coming out of college. Our star recruit proved worthy in every way imaginable. He not only leveraged the training and work experience professionally, but has become a highly-respected leader and volunteer in the community at large. I am proud to recognize my brother for helping making this project a reality.

There were many others both in and outside of my firm who too made valuable contributions to this endeavor. My senior associate, Keith Price, assumed a portion of my day-to-day office responsibilities in order to afford me spare time on the job to finish writing. I also would be remiss not to recognize Stanley Tucker and other partners of MMG Ventures. By hiring me to facilitate an entrepreneurial training for many of their portfolio clients I had the opportunity to teach and test my teaching concepts and methods about financial management.

INTRODUCTION

Cultivating a profitable business is not always linked to the skills or educational training a business owner or decision-maker receives in school. Many secrets of success lie in the application and exercise of judgment in real time and under pressure. In this view, monetizing ideas, knowledge and expertise is the single most daunting challenge for entrepreneurs and business owners. In order to be successful financially they must develop, package and market a product or service to customers willing to pay a price above cost.

After a marketable product or service has been successfully promoted proficiency in financial management usually separates the winners and losers. Skill and seasoned judgment in financial management is required to effectively navigate the ebbs and flow of an ever changing and fluctuating economic landscape. As a failsafe every business should install and rely on a sound system of financial management techniques, tactics and strategies.

Whether you are seasoned, newly minted or an aspiring business owner it is important to ask yourself some basic questions. Namely, are you overly dependent on your accountants to understand the meaning of the financial data? Have you ever been shocked by a potential investor's unfavorable conclusion about the financial strengths and weaknesses of your business? Do you feel uncomfortable navigating between different financial statements?

Are you unable to identify critical financial information for your business? Do you struggle to convert profit potential into real financial returns? Is cash flow a chronic and crippling problem? Is your legal infrastructure weak and ill-fitted to your business model?

Road to MegaSuccess

If you answer in the affirmative to any of the questions above, *The Road to MegaSuccess* may be your best solution. This book is tailored for the entrepreneur who has experienced anxiety, frustration, or trauma in building a financially viable business. It demystifies the conventional financial methods of business management, so that the average person without a financial background can easily understand. Deliberately designed to be an easy read, this book will help to increase the odds for your business success.

Perplexing financial challenges and risks are buried beneath the surface of virtually every business opportunity. Because circumstances and conditions are not always 100% controllable it is critical to devise a financial plan that is adaptable. You also have to master the skills required to identify and carefully manage the bottom line. To this end, in this book we teach practical concepts, techniques and methods for building and sustaining a profitable business. The framework is presented and explained from an entrepreneurial perspective.

I also discuss ways to make, measure, account and grow money by leveraging your financial resources. The focal point is on helping you devise a fundamental set of financial management practices to achieve a positive bottom line on a consistent basis. Sustaining profits over the long haul is key to maintaining a healthy business.

Most entrepreneurs start with a relatively limited capital base. This makes for a small margin for error. Rather than flirt with loss of capital it is better to acquire knowledge and skill in the use, application and reporting of financial resources vicariously rather than through actual experience. Self-starters cannot afford to make an expensive error in judgment and expect to recover financially. With these constraints in mind business owners must be vigilant in finding the best way to maximize return on investment.

By becoming actively involved in the financial management of your business prospects for success are much higher. The survival rate is low for armchair spectators who leave financial decision making solely to their accountants, managers or consultants. With this in mind, the aim of The Road to MegaSuccess is to strengthen entrepreneurs' financial capabilities as well as reveal potentially fatal hazards.

Just as preparation and discipline are germane to the ultimate success of a pro athlete and the team, sound financial management can elevate business performance. Many pro athletes recognized long ago that to get to the top of their respective sports—be it the Super Bowl, the Stanley Cup, the NBA Finals, or the Masters—personal development and self-improvement must be part of their everyday lives. Most successful entrepreneurs also recognize that their overall success is directly tied to how well their companies are prepared to perform and operate financially.

Enriching the Bottom Line

Some of the most fundamental techniques used to improve business earnings are relatively straightforward. Quite often these principles are based on life experience. We will highlight and make these associations while illustrating proven methods for maximizing profitability, cash flow and net worth. Likewise, case studies involving well known successful enterprises will be used to demonstrate management solutions that work well for large as well as small companies.

Our study will start with the most common financial difficulties entrepreneurs typically encounter. You will walk in the shoes of seasoned business veterans as they search out ways to formulate effective financial strategies and solutions. The journey stretches from the infancy to maturity stages of business life.

Detailed attention is paid to plotting financial DNA including the timing and flow of incoming and outgoing dollars—whether invested, borrowed, or earned. Guidance will be provided based on the premise that any business leader who does not know or track the flow of dollars is destined to under-perform or, worse, fail. With this in mind entrepreneurs, aspirants, CEOs, and managers should find the step by step rollout of information extremely valuable.

Rest assured, in order to master the fundamentals you need not be a mathematician or Certified Public Accountant. In this book, a dozen chapter titles express the thrust of what I describe as, *Simple Strategies for Enriching the Bottom Line.* These keys are widely embraced by investors, bankers, and other professionals who routinely advise business owners. Perhaps more important, they offer a road map for keeping a business in tip top shape financially.

The range of tools introduced span from short-hand methods of determining breakeven to determining the financing needs of your business. These skills are crucial for every business owner to keep their business afloat and attract capital for growth.

Profitable Growth Management

A common business objective shared by virtually every company is growth. With size the hope is for greater financial muscle, which in turn presumably leads to greater efficiency and higher profits. To a fault some businesses think of growth and profitability as being mutually exclusive. On the contrary, a sound strategic plan gives equal weight to growth and profitability.

Intuitively most business people think of growth without fully recognizing the many financial challenges that come along. Growth is typically thought of singularly as increased sales, more locations, larger staff, additional equipment and higher financing requirements. Far too often a detailed analysis of any associated profit or lack thereof is placed on the backburner.

When a business loses focus on profitability, growth can be financially counterproductive. The effects may include cash short fall, inability to secure credit and lack of funding to introduce new products and services. Many entrepreneurs quickly learn the hard way that growth that results in decreasing profits can harmful. To avoid the pitfall every business needs a well-conceived plan calculated to produce profitable growth.

Accelerating the Journey

In order to help understand the fundamental financial concepts and methods underlying profitable growth the book highlights applicable parts of a practical case study at the beginning of each chapter. The journey is depicted through the eyes of two fictional entrepreneurs BJ Armstrong and Taylor Made should resonate with self-starters and seasoned business pros. Their plight is a common one which you should find easy to understand.

Just as important as having a case study reference we provide simple numeric applications. These basic illustrations are included to provide examples of practical applications. After putting these simulations in context you will undoubtedly discover that memorizing numbers, balances, or figures, is by no means essential to achieving high financial returns. In fact, very few highly successful entrepreneurs expound detailed financial information contained in the body of their company's financial statements. On the other hand, they have a commanding knowledge and grasp of the fundamental financial parameters of their business.

Rarely will a banker or investor be inclined to invest capital in a company unless the CEO has a thorough understanding of the finances of their business. With rare exception, entrepreneurs have to be prepared to run the gamut of financial options and when necessary, have enough insight to explain the financial performance and condition of their company.

In the final analysis, you need not be a financial expert to be successful in business. However, the odds are much greater for those able to interpret basic financial statements and comprehend their meaning. Accordingly, the goal of this book is to provide a simple Roadmap to help enrich the bottom line for any business or industry. To keep on track you'll learn to rely on a twelve point mantra highlighted on the back cover.

On first thought, the idea of reading a book about how to improve the bottom line may seem a bit intimidating, if not overwhelming. However, you need not worry, as each of the topics will be reduced to simple common principles like those we live and use to make every day personal financial decisions. I am confident the journey you are about to take will leave you better equipped to accelerate profitably along T*he Road to MegaSuccess.*

CHAPTER ONE

Start at Home... The Financial Foundation

| *The Journey* |

AFTER TEN YEARS IN THE WORKFORCE, BJ Armstrong launched his own business. He named it Mediclean Corporation. Mediclean Corporation distributes housekeeping, cleaning, and maintenance supplies to health care facilities. Its products include detergents, waxes, and other industrial cleansers. Mediclean also sells restaurant and dining room supplies—such as glasses, tableware, napkins, and coffeepot filters. Several years ago, the company decided to offer customers a complete solution under one roof. Accordingly, it started a commercial maintenance and cleaning services division within the company.

In order to grow the business BJ needs an injection of capital. He plans to review his personal finances to determine just how much additional cash he can afford to contribute to his business. He is inclined to consider personal options before seeking an investor, business partner or bank loan to fund his planned expansion.

BJ has significant personal assets. He owns several residential rental properties. However, he operates slightly in the red on a monthly basis which has made it difficult to save money. Making matters worse, BJ has run up several credit card accounts to maximum limit.

If you can relate to any part of BJ's personal financial situation, this Chapter will help you to exercise better control over your personal finances. Building a profitable business starts first with strengthening your household enterprise.

In the early stages of development most businesses are funded by owners with personal funds. These financial means commonly come from personal savings and investments as well as home equity line of credit. Contrary to popular impression a pivotal factor for success in business is a function of their odds for success depend as much on the quality of financial management at home.

CHAPTER HIGHLIGHTS

- Personal Financial Management
- Monitoring Household Income and Expenses
- Achieving Financial Equilibrium
- Saving for a Rainy Day
- Investing Wisely

Operation Bootstrap

Over the long term, running your household or business by your bootstraps is no way to achieve financial Mega-Success. To this point have you ever found yourself buried in a financial quagmire… with no foreseeable source of free money? Are you virtually forced to rob Peter to pay Paul? If so, or even if you have found yourself close, rest assured you are not alone.

Life often throws curve balls at us that have the potential to skew a predetermined pathway. How you choose to navigate these unexpected situations can have a lasting impact on personal financial health and wellness. Ultimately, your response to financial distress determines whether your short and long-term financial goals come to fruition.

Far too often when people are faced with overwhelming financial stress, they turn to bootstrapping. Common examples of personal bootstrapping include borrowing against your retirement fund or cash surrender value of insurance, paying off income tax liabilities using a credit card, and covering routine household bills though a home equity line of credit.

Bootstrapping is just as prevalent in the business world. While ill advised, some business owners dip into payroll withholding money to meet current payroll, regularly pay vendors on a delinquent basis, or borrow money from nontraditional lenders at grossly overpriced rates of interest. Let's be completely honest. At one time or another, most of us have been guilty of bootstrapping on one level or another.

Frankly, it is very difficult not to succumb to bootstrapping especially on a personal level. Even for a highly disciplined person, the gravity of life's conundrums pulls you in. They range from private school or college tuition payments, down payment on the purchase of a home, or a payment of medical insurance deductible. Often, it seems financial crises arise at the worst possible times. At any level of income it becomes difficult if not impossible to absorb the impact of unplanned cash expenditures.

In plotting financial strategy, one might wonder whether it is wise to bootstrap the operations of a business or personal enterprise. The simple answer is, it is not sustainable and therefore, not in your long term best interest. Bootstrapping on a continuous basis risk irreparable harm to your financial reputation, credit history and long standing relationships. Ultimately, bootstrapping may be a precursor to insolvency, which is a financial condition where you are no longer able to pay your debts.

The best way to financially protect your household from the perils of bootstrapping is not only to plan to develop a sound financial plan, but also to methodically monitor it. While this book primarily focuses on proactive financial business management, this chapter will examine some the most effective steps to take to keep your personal financial affairs in order. Remember, for most small business owners, personal and business finances are intricately connected.

Undoubtedly, there will be occasions when you make a financial decision that later proves to be a mistake. Fortunately, in most cases there will be ample time to recover either by cutting back or reprioritizing future expenditures. Another solution may be to devise a way to generate more income. The key to rebuilding is to learn from and avoid repeating the same mistake.

Bootstrapping poses the risk of irreparable harm to your financial standing

The techniques for managing household finances are not significantly different from techniques used to generate profit for a small business. Ideally, you sketch out

Plan A, your intended actions, and Plan B, the plan you will implement should conditions not materialize as expected. Next, you should document key assumptions regarding income and expense under each scenario. Lastly, determine your options for controlling, eliminating or compensating for any deviations from the budget along the way.

For it to have maximum use and value a financial plan for a business or personal enterprise should be flexible. It should be developed with the understanding that circumstances will probably arise that were not anticipated. Sometimes these unexpected developments involve job loss, pay cut or escalation in cost of personal insurance. Therefore, it is wise to build in a cushion. On the other hand, there are future activities that will be far more manageable in terms of cost such as a wedding, education and vacation. A good plan takes into account the expected and creates an allowance for the unexpected.

Sound financial preparation also takes into account external economic trends and developments. For instance, rising interest rates on home mortgage, credit cards, and student loans have to be incorporated into your financial plan. Ignoring these trends raises the risk that you will fall short of your financial goals. In the final analysis, a well-conceived financial plan sets specific targets and lays out a series of action steps necessary to get there.

Personal Surveillance

Effective personal financial management is linked to ongoing oversight. Essentially, oversight involves monitoring your personal finances including earnings, money spent, as well as lifestyle changes that have financial impact. With lifestyle variation comes the need to make adjustments and revisions to help remain within the boundaries of your financial plan. Furthermore, if it is not updated routinely, your financial plan like a business plan, will become obsolete.

Technology provides a convenient way to facilitate money management. For instance, with the aid of technology, it is simple to automate transfers from primary to savings and retirement accounts. Likewise, through online banking, it is easy to schedule bill, credit card and loan payments. Doing so will help you avoid late fees and further damage to your credit. These parts of a business or personal financial plan should be automated to the maximum extent possible.

It is helpful to categorize similar types of expenses, funding and income sources. Doing so helps you review and assess the direction of your income and expenses. For example, a designated special occasion fund could serve as a savings tool and budget control measure for planned vacations, trips and other special events. A separate account also is recommended for owners of income producing rental property to deposit rents and pay expenses. An indirect but important benefit of this organizational approach is the creation of a well defined audit trail that can easily be monitored.

Use automated bank transfers, alerts and other controls to keep on track with your financial plan

There is no distinction between business and personal financial management when it comes to optimizing cash flow. In both cases, the end game is for cash inflows to match or exceed cash outflows.

The science behind managing cash flow lies in forecasting needs and requirements on a monthly basis over a twelve month period. This is essentially a short-term budget management process that seeks to avoid bank account overdrafts, late payments and related penalties.

The cash flow evaluation process should start with itemizing the normal monthly flow of cash inflows and outflows. Next, you should flow chart any anticipated balloon payments such as security deposits as well as windfalls from insurance claims. Mapping out anomalies before they happen and making up a plan in advance is a sign of effective cash flow management.

For analytical purposes, it may be convenient to break out inflows and outflows of cash in two columns—namely, recurring and nonrecurring cash activities. You may identify discretionary versus non-discretionary cash inflows and outflows within each group. This will make it easy to categorize your expenses. In essence, you should separate your regular monthly household expenses and debt payments—which are often tied to mortgages, automobiles, education loans and other debt obligations—from your discretionary cash expenditures. Discretionary cash expenditures may include entertainment and social costs. If ever you fall into a cash crunch, this makes it much easier to prioritize and slash where necessary.

Effective cash flow management maintains equilibrium between cash inflows and outflows

When cash flow management serves its purpose, the end product is free cash at the end of the month. In turn, you can plow that cash into your savings and investments. You will relieve yourself of the pressures of heavy cash outflow. Also, you will be less tempted to borrow against credit cards, home equity lines of credit and other personal debt that lingers. Remember, effective cash flow management should improve financial decision making and help control your personal spending.

Spending Caps

A common shared goal in both personal and business life is to make dollars earned stretch further. Many of us lament based on money earned that there never seems to be any left over. Reviewing how your money is spent is a logical starting point.

An old adage speaks volumes, it's not always how much you make but how much you keep. Wayward personal spending is a major impediment to building a nest egg. Uncontrolled spending disrupts a well-laid financial plan and over time may break the human will to live by a financial budget. In essence, spending without any point of reference runs the risk of becoming habit forming. This is especially true when the money fueling the spending is tied to a one-time windfall such as the lottery, inheritance or legal settlement. Beware.

For some people, access to open ended debt financing can be a financial downfall. It's tempting to continually dip into a home equity line of credit and cash advances on a credit card to cover routine expenses. In these situations, the need to cut back spending and conserve is masked. Other telltale signs of wayward spending include spending—rather than rolling over pension funds—or depleting, rather than reinvesting, a lump sum distribution from a pension fund.

Unharnessed personal spending becomes habitual overspending

Fortunately, our financial system invokes some involuntary spending controls. Many times as part of the loan underwriting process, they will objectively evaluate a person's ability to make financial repayments. One of the most well established lending criteria is one's ability to repay his or her monthly mortgage. The widely held standard is that a family's monthly mortgage payment should not exceed 30% to 40% of household income. Where the size of a mortgage puts the prospective borrower over the limit, the lender usually declines the applicant. So, if the size of the monthly mortgage you seek exceeds your household income by more than 30% or 40%, the lender will likely decline your application.

On the other hand, adherence to such a benchmark is still no guarantee your financial decision was wise even when you qualify for a big-ticket loan such as a mortgage. For instance, it may be feasible to spend 40% of your household income on mortgage payments now, but unmanageable in five years with two children attending college. In hindsight what looked to be a sound financial decision could be disastrous later. In the final analysis, you have to protect yourself from financially overextending yourself.

If you find your poor personal spending habits have already landed you in a minefield of financial distress, do not give up hope. Recovery and rebuilding is possible through effective debt restructure and spending reductions. For instance, some relief may be achieved from refinancing your mortgage at a lower interest rate or extending the term of the mortgage. Either way provides a path for lowering your monthly mortgage payment. Likewise, debt consolidation—as in, consolidating your home equity line of credit and an existing mortgage into a simple loan—could also be beneficial.

When confronted with spiraling consumer debt largely driven by escalating interest, consider switching your credit card provider. It may allow you to take advantage of lower interest rates. Occasionally, banks offer promotions to attract balance transfers with moratorium on payments for a specific span of time. However, a word of caution is warranted here: renegotiating outstanding credit can damage your credit rating if not handled properly. Consult an expert before making any significant financial decisions. Beware.

In order to prepare for a prosperous financial future, concentrate on managing and reducing debt so that payments are well below the standards lenders consider ordinary and customary. The next section of the chapter provides specific guidance on how to financially prepare for the unexpected.

Stash of Cash

With insurance coverage not being offered for every risk and contingency, how can you possibly prepare for unexpected financial outlays and setbacks? Most financial professionals agree that the best way to defend against the unexpected is to maintain a stash of cash.

Whether speaking about a household or business enterprise, setting an adequate amount of money for a rainy day is crucial to survival. It's impossible for anyone to completely guard himself or herself against every financial risk. I'm speaking about those financial risks that have the potential to cause a full-scale financial meltdown. Fortunately, there is a way to weather the storm. The question is, "Do you have the financial muscle to withstand a heavy blow and bounce back?"

To answer the question, take a page from the banking industry. Financial stress testing is now mandatory throughout the banking industry. This applies both to so called "big" and "medium" banking institutions. In many ways, this process has served to forewarn individual banks and helped to stabilize our banking system overall. That said, I advise you to incorporate your own personal financial stress test. Create your own way to test your personal financial stress and build that into your personal financial planning process.

Start by drilling yourself on some basic questions. Are your cash reserves sufficient to absorb an unexpected expense of $3,000? If for any reason your paychecks stop for two pay periods, could you continue to pay your home mortgage and other routine household expenses? Will your cash reserves cover deductibles on life, health, disability and long term care insurance? Knowing you have the financial capacity to survive unexpected, but not impossible, financial difficulties is an indication of your financial health.

The truth is most professionals rarely agree about the exact amount of money a family should keep on reserve. However, most do agree that in today's economy, it is wise for the average family to have enough money to cover six to nine months of living expenses. Typically, this reserve is referred to as an emergency fund.

Whether or not you are an entrepreneur, a family emergency fund is crucial to insure your household has the financial strength to endure and recover from a major financial shock. In today's world, disruptions caused by unexpected events—such as job loss, medical and family emergencies—are common.

At a minimum your emergency fund should be sufficient to cover six to nine months cost of living.

Every family should determine how much money they

should keep in their emergency fund. Each family will differ with respect to what it requires as a safe amount. There are many important factors to consider. They include household composition and income sources. For example, a single person who is completely self-reliant may need a much greater cushion than a couple with two streams of income. Likewise, if you are employed in an industry on the decline or at risk for significant job reductions, you should increase your emergency fund. This will allow for greater coverage. Health issues, job training and number of family dependents also are pertinent to establishing your emergency fund targets.

In the final analysis, there is no hard and fast rule for setting the requisite amount for your emergency fund. The target should be based on your household, family and financial circumstances rather than a rigid yardstick. Be flexible.

Self-Control

Now that we've instilled the importance of building up your emergency fund, it's time to turn to growing your personal wealth fund. A wealth fund covers all assets including cash, personal and real property of any nature. Accordingly, your wealth fund will include a home, car, patent, copyright, stocks, bonds, mutual funds as well as retirement assets. A wealth fund extends to jewelry, time-share properties, farmland, leases and assets of all kinds.

Self-control is the primary, nontechnical skill required for building wealth. A helpful mantra is: spend less, make more, and invest the difference. The bedrock of a wealth-building plan is the commitment and discipline to do the following: spend below your means, earn more than you absolutely need to live on and make prudent investments.

For most of us, the pathway to building wealth hinges on defeating wayward spending. The best way to combat this tendency is to establish rigid spending benchmarks. Recall, we learned mortgage lenders generally agree that households should spend no more than 30% to 40% of their income on a monthly mortgage. Other authors suggest we grow to accept and abide by another rigid criteria: a household should spend no more than 90% of income for the total cost of

The key to honing personal wealth is discipline. Spend less, make more, and investing the difference

living. This 90% includes mortgage, utilities, food, medical expenses, entertainment and other expenses. Under this model, you will automatically generate a residual of 10% to apply to your to savings and investing.

To illustrate the virtues of a 90-10 saving-spending rule, compare the finances of two people: Karen and Jake. Both Karen and Jake bring home a monthly income of $1,000. Karen spends no more than 90% of her monthly income and saves $100 monthly. Two years later, when her monthly income increases to $2,000, Karen continues to save based on 10% guideline. As a result, Karen begins to add $200 monthly to her nest egg. In essence, her wealth grows in proportion to income.

Jake, on the other hand, starts to save $100 monthly on $1,000 monthly income. Jake decides to tie his budgeted savings solely to an absolute dollar figure of $100. Assume Jake's month income grows to $2,000 two-years later. Jake's savings rate will crepe along much slower than Karen's saving rate. This means Jake will save less money than Karen. Don't be Jake. Be Karen. As our example illustrates, it is more important to establish a savings rate than a specific savings amount.

The 90 - 10 spend to save ratio not only serves to control personal spending, but also helps to establish a savings habit. If a 30-year old contributes 10% of his $60,000 annual salary to a tax deferred retirement savings account, it could grow to $1.2 million by age 65 (assuming an average 7% rate of return and 3% annual pay raise).

Unlike traditional budgeting, the spend-save rule does not specify how and where you should spend 90% of your hard earned money. Where you spend that 90% is left to your discretion. You should customize and prioritize your spending to fit your life style and preferences. In other words, the spend-save rule preservers your autonomy in terms choice of personal spending.

If you follow the spend-save rule of thumb, then your saving at minimum will equal one year's salary in just a few years. However, even achieving this milestone will not finish the job. The conventional wisdom today is that most people will require between seven and ten times their annual salary to live comfortably in retirement. Entrepreneurship has the potential to fill in any remaining gap.

Budget to spend no more than 90% of your income on the cost of living and apply the remaining 10% to saving

Time Line

Regrettably, most people do not start saving soon enough to build up their financial coffers in time for retirement. A key objective for most personal financial plans is to squirrel away enough money to allow you to live your golden years without having to work full time or be reliant on family for financial support.

A 30-year old who adopts the spend-save model and continues saving to age 65, should meet their retirement savings objective by retirement age. However, the fate of people who delay savings until their 40s, 50s or 60s is far less certain. With significantly less than 35 years for their savings to accumulate and investments to grow, they may have to make adjustments to the spend-save model to accelerate wealth building.

Fortunately, the spending - save rule is adaptable. To make up ground in a hurry, late bloomers should consider increasing their save rate by 5% every 5 years. Rather than simply using a 90-10 save to spend-save ratio, it may be appropriate to escalate the spend-save ratio to 85-15 after five years, then to 80-20 in another five years. These periodic realignments should enable a person 45-years old to catch up to the 30-year old's saving level by age 65. If your retirement timeline is less than 15 years, you may require more frequent adjustments.

At the end of the day, the sooner you begin saving and investing the larger your nest egg has the potential to grow. Regular consistent savings is not the only tool you should rely on to cross the finish line. Further enhancing your savings rate may call for additional measures.

Roll Back

Depending on the stage of life when you begin squirreling away money for the future, it may be important to supplement your regular income in order to meet your current and long-term financial goals.

In the business world, roll backs often mean a sell off of a company's least productive assets or replacing debt funds with investor funds. If roll backs are used in business to retrench and squeeze out cash buried in certain business assets, you might ask why not apply the same technique to help the recovery of a household enterprise?

Save early and often, especially if you just started to squirrel away money for retirement.

Under certain circumstances, a roll back can serve to nurse the finances of household back to good health. Naturally, this course of action will involve making less than desirable compromises and sacrifices for long term good. For example, if you wish to reduce your personal debt and provide more breathing room to pay living expenses, you will need to limit your discretionary spending. It could further be necessary to liquidate certain personal assets to generate cash funds. Whether it pertains to personal or real property assets, recapitalizing your household often boils down to a simple commitment: determine what you could afford to live without.

Disposable personal and real property could range from undeveloped land and vacation homes to a second automobile, boat and any other item of personal property of a non-essential nature. In essence, asset liquidation may be the only viable solution to getting your cash flow and financial savings plan on track.

In some instances, the financial impact of recapitalizing has a positive income tax benefit. For example, after consulting your own CPA about the tax effects of capital gains and losses, you may discover under current law gain on the sale of your principal residence up to a defined limit is exempt from taxation. Therefore, one roll back option is to sell one home and reinvest in another more affordable home. You'll have the advantage of having some portion of the proceeds put into your pocket.

On the other hand, you also can choose to leverage the equity in your home to fund your retirement without having to sell your house. Presently, there are tax incentives that promote holding onto your principal residence and aging in place. Specifically, for a person 62 years of age and older, a reverse mortgage allows you to borrow or draw down cash based on the equity in your home, while you retain possession and occupancy. A reverse mortgage is essentially a hybrid form of asset liquidation. In exchange for a promise to pay back someday in the future, money is freed up to live on today. Check with your CPA regarding the tax implications based on your specific financial situation.

Strategically liquidate nonessential assets to pay down debt and boost savings for investment

Arguably the next most important step to consider in recovering financially and building up your wealth fund is formulating a sustainable strategy to earn more money.

Your Side Hustle

Income from a side hustle may be integral to a wealth building strategy. There are multitudes of ways to side hustle. Namely, upgrade your hobby to a side hustle. These hobbies could include tutoring, freelancing and moonlighting. Ideally, the side hustle you cultivate will have the potential to turn into a full fledge business venture.

While this book is designed to provide financial management guidance for developing a profitable business enterprise, there are many parallels to draw in relation to a side hustle. Most notable, the aim is to get best value possible for services rendered. Hustle hard. Hustle smart.

At first, newbies in search for a side hustle tend to undervalue their skills, talent and experience. This may be necessary to get your foot in the door. However, just as any proprietor, it makes sense to test the waters. Side gigs are mostly about making extra money, not building a professionally fulfilling career.

A major pocket for side hustle opportunities can be found with respect to today's so called "shared economy". The fundamental concept refers to "peer to peer based" sharing of access to goods and services. These are mostly coordinated through online marketing platforms. The opportunities to land side hustles have a wide range of possibilities. Find your hustle. Share your hustle.

The most well recognized peer-to-peer bargaining includes ride sharing, room rentals, baby-sitting and home moving services. Over time, your options are bound to grow.

Much like any other business opportunity, shared peer-to-peer bargaining sets the stage for shared creation, production, distribution, trade and consumption of goods and services. It is virtually certain that there are needs that match your skills, experience and talent. Virtually anyone can sign up. Push your hustle to the masses.

Many of these platforms are constructed to meet a variety of needs including adjunct teaching, event planning, tutoring, catering and professional assistance. The discretion to make your own decisions and control your own schedule closely resembles the operating framework of an entrepreneur. In this sense, this work experience is great preparation for starting a full fledge business enterprise.

Supplement your income through the shared economy.

Of course, there are many other more traditional ways to supplement your income. Alternatives include taking on a second job, signing on for part time work, and working overtime with your primary employer. There also are a wide variety of special online project opportunities, such as voice-overs, online marketing assistance and virtual assistant business. Be creative with your hustle.

Market your skills, experience and talent online.

In essence, you can leverage a side hustle to help reduce debt, pay down expenses and ultimately, to build up your wealth fund. At the same time you will learn entrepreneurship skills that could lead to inventing a new product, invention, or service that can be marketed for profit.

As the discussion suggests, when your financial planning calls for making more money in addition to cutting back expenses, there are plenty of opportunities to make this happen. Equipped with viable strategies to make extra money, the next section provides guidance on how and where to invest your hard earned cash.

Asset Mix

Having extolled the virtues of money management from an income and expense perspective, we now turn to ways for deciding where and how to invest your financial resources. Conventional wisdom is that too much concentration in one type of asset poses significant risks, while asset diversification is more prudent.

Your asset mix should be reviewed periodically to insure the right balance of liquidity.

From a risk management viewpoint, it is important to avoid tying up too much of your assets into retirement funds, annuities, real estate or nonmarketable stocks and bonds. Doing so concentrates illiquid assets in excess. This poses the risk of financial insolvency. In essence, you might find yourself without enough liquid assets to pay liabilities when due. Accordingly, it is wise to maintain a diversified portfolio of both liquid and non-liquid assets.

Aside from investment risk, liquidity of different assets should be a key concern with regard to deciding where to invest your financial resources.

Liquidity refers to ability to convert an asset into cash and the freedom to use your money as needed. Preferably, in the context of liquidity, your asset mix should be aligned with future financial needs and requirements as they mature.

In many respects asset mixture or balance is driven by liquidity considerations. If anything, we understand emergencies often call for easy access to cash. Recall our previous discussion about establishing an emergency fund. Beyond the need to be liquid just in case of emergencies, asset liquidity should correlate to other future events and contingencies. For example, it is wise to schedule investment liquidity to correspond to payment of college tuition, down payment on a home and income needed for support during retirement. Keeping your asset balance in check requires taking a forward look at life's journey. Folks, it's time we look ahead.

For instance, take a person at age 50 may forecast retirement in 20 years. She may plan to start liquidating investments set aside for retirement at that time to help cover living expenses. Logistically speaking under these circumstances selection of investments may very well be tilted to maximize returns over a twenty-year period with the goal to mature by the end of the twenty-year investment cycle. Maximizing returns on investment is no more important than liquidity. In fact, it may be necessary to cash out earlier than twenty years, and if so, proper planning will insure the investments will be saleable.

By simple illustration one tier of this person's asset mix might include municipal bonds with a 20-year maturity date. By contrast, a parent expecting a child to enter college in five years may choose treasury bills, money market funds or other short term investment alternatives.

Generally, it is best to seek professional input and guidance when selecting investments to insure choices that fit your particular needs and circumstances. In addition to level of expected return there are other important criteria. For instance, the concept of volatility is paramount. Volatility refers to how cash-out values tend to fluctuate overtime with respect to certain types of investments. Cash-out values on various assets could be high or low. Volatility is simply the term we use to describe those variations.

Your wealth fund should be comprised of a diversified portfolio of investments.

In order to meet certain future needs, an investment prone to a high degree of volatility may not be desirable even if it offers potential for a relatively high rate of return. For example, assume you make a financial investment to pay for college education in five years. Or, assume you make a financial investment to fund your retirement next year. Ordinarily, these investments would not be suitable for an investment known to have a high probability to fluctuate in value. In truth, any type of investment has the potential to be volatile and thus caution should be exercised.

Liquidity and volatility can sometimes work in opposite directions. For instance, stocks traded on the New York Stock Exchange may be highly liquid but also, subject to a high degree of volatility. If you need to cash out when the stock is selling at a low point, you could be short of your original investment and expected capital gain. Significant swings in a bond's value can occur as short-term interest rates move back and forth.

On the other hand, some investors regard real estate as less risky in terms volatility, but far less liquid than market traded stocks and bonds. Generally speaking while real estate values may not be as prone to vary widely daily, it may takes weeks, months or years to sale. For financial planning purposes, it is helpful to weigh the inherent risk of the investment itself along with the other collateral concerns mentioned.

Liquidity and volatility sometimes work in opposition

Parking Options

There are plenty of options for saving and investing money. Think of options for saving and investing money as vehicles. These vehicles come in many varieties whereby the investment product is self-managed, professionally managed or managed by reference to a stock exchange. Ultimately most investing will be based on your appetite for risk, expectation for returns and need for security.

A "portfolio" is the collection of investments held by you or an investment company or financial institution. It is common for investors to maintain portfolios at all three levels. However, I assure you what is comfortable and appropriate for one individual may not be satisfactory for someone else. Your portfolio is unique to you and you alone.

Liquidity, risk and volatility should be carefully evaluated when selecting investments.

Each person has their own set of needs, requirements and comfort levels with respect to investments. As a broad reference some of the most common investment vehicles are itemized below:

Short Term Options

Savings Account

A simple savings account is one of the most commonly used tools through which investors can earn interest on their money. Banks and credit unions offer a variety of savings vehicles, each with varying requirements and levels of return. Basic savings accounts are the most liquid type of investment, and deposits are backed by the Federal Deposit Insurance Corporation for balances up to $250,000.

Money Markey Account

A money market account is a specialized type of savings account that usually earns a greater amount of interest than a basic savings account. The minimum balance for this account is generally considerably higher than the minimum balance on a basic savings account. Some money market accounts also have limited check writing and debit card features. They offer the same bank protection as a savings account.

Certificates of Deposit

A certificate of deposit (CD) is a time deposit similar to a savings account. A CD bears a maturity date (ranging from 30 days to five years), a specified fixed interest rate (typically greater than that for a basic savings account) and can be issued in any amount. CDs are beneficial for people who know they will not need access to their cash for a specific period of time. CDs are generally issued by commercial banks and insured by the Federal Deposit Insurance Corporation.

Intermediate and Long Term Options

Generally intermediate length investments of five to ten years are tied to a balanced portfolio of stocks and bonds. This affords the best of both worlds between dividends, capital gains and interest. Vehicles commonly used for this type of investing include:

Mutual Funds

A mutual fund is a company that pools money from many investors and invests the money in securities such as stocks, bonds and short-term debt. The combined holdings of a mutual fund are known as its portfolio. Investors buy shares in mutual funds. Each share represents an investor's part of ownership in the fund and the income it generates. Mutual funds generally are professionally managed, offer diversification, require minimum investment and can easily be redeemed at any time for the current net asset value. On the other hand, with mutual funds, you could lose all or some of the money you invest because securities held by the fund can go down.

Stock

A stock is an ownership share in a corporation. As you acquire more stock your ownership stake in the company increases. The term "share equity" and "stock" are used interchangeably. Stock conveys a claim on the company's assets and earnings. The value of stock is subject to fluctuation and thus puts your investment at risk. On the other hand, stock potentially offers the highest rate of return over an extended period of time.

Bonds

Bonds are loans. Essentially an investor serves as the bank. You can loan money in the form of a bond to a company, a city, or the government. In exchange for a loan the borrower promises to pay the bank back in full, with regular interest payments. Interest rates may be fixed or variable over a defined period of time. Bonds are issued in multiples of $1,000 usually for periods of five to twenty years. Their market value depends mainly on the rating awarded by bond rating agencies and based on the issuer's reputation and financial strength. Bonds, like other investments, put your money at varying degrees of risk for devaluation and loss of principle.

Taxwise Investing

Rarely will a single account at one bank or brokerage house an investor's entire portfolio. In fact, the conventional wisdom is that you should not choose to put all your eggs in one basket. Likewise, with respect to designated saving account variety has benefit according to intended use, such as for retirement, health care, or college. The different accounts offer varying degrees of tax incentives, such as deferral of income taxes on returns until funds are withdrawn, tax deductible contributions to investment accounts, and tax free treatment of investment earnings. Eligibility for these tax breaks generally depends on income, household composition and other criteria. Accordingly, you should consult with a tax professional when evaluating the various possibilities. A brief synopsis of the most common tax efficient savings alternatives are outlined below:

Traditional IRA

A traditional individual retirement aaccount is a personal savings plan that allows you to accumulate money tax deferred. The extent to which contributions are tax deductible depends on your income level and whether you or your spouse participates in an employer retirement plan. There is a limitation on the amount of annual contributions to a traditional IRA. The earnings on a Traditional IRA are taxed when they are distributed.

ROTH IRA

While similar in nature to a traditional IRA, there are some striking differences between a Traditional and ROTH IRA. With a ROTH IRA you pay taxes on money going into your account, and then all future withdrawals are tax free. Because the money you save is not tax subsidized, you can tap your contributions (but not your earnings) tax-free and penalty-free at any time. Like a Traditional IRA, there are limitations on annual contributions to ROTH IRAs.

401k

A 401k is a retirement savings plan sponsored by an employer. It allows the employee to save and invest a portion of his paycheck before taxes are taken out. Taxes are not paid until the money is taken out of the account. The annual contribution limits are much higher than allowed for a Traditional or ROTH IRA.

Simplified Employee Pension (SEP)

A SEP is retirement arrangement that allows an employer to make contributions to a Traditional IRA (SEP IRA) for each eligible employee. The limits on employer contributions to a SEP IRA are generally higher than the limits on Traditional or ROTH IRAs SEPs are popular with self-employed individuals, because they have the same contribution limits as profit sharing plans without the complex compliance and reporting rules.

Health Savings Account (HSA)

A HSA is a tax-advantaged medical savings account. HSA contributions can be drawn on tax free to pay for certain medical expenses, such as out-of-pocket medical, dental, and vision costs. HSAs are not allowed to be used to pay insurance premiums, and they can only be used with "High Deductible Health Plans." Lastly, all funds put in and HSA are 100% tax deductible; however, there are limits to the amount of money you can contribute annually.

The tools used to manage your personal finances and build personal wealth are similar to the techniques used by businesses to build value. Similarly, the success you have in managing your personal financial affairs usually has a direct bearing on the level of success achieved in operating a business enterprise. That said, the next chapter will focus on the common pitfalls entrepreneurs should avoid at the business enterprise level.

NOTABLE REFLECTIONS AT A GLANCE

- Building a successful business starts from home with a personal financial plan for closely monitoring household finances.
- Bootstrapping usually can be eliminated with more effective management of your personal finances.
- Undisciplined personal spending puts your personal financial equilibrium in jeopardy.
- Personal financial planning requires navigating cash inflows and outflows.
- Don't leave home without an Emergency Fund.
- Building wealth comes through spending less, making more and investing the difference.

CHAPTER TWO

Set the Right Course... Prepare for MegaSuccess

| *The Journey* |

LIKE MOST ENTREPRENEURS, BJ struggled to survive during his initial years of business. It was difficult to produce a positive cash flow. Earning consistent, bottom line profit was also challenging. For the first two years, BJ's expenses outpaced his revenues. In the third year, when the company finally generated a profit, cash flow became erratic and unpredictable. As a result, payments to suppliers frequently fell behind. This jeopardized the company's credit standing. Luckily for BJ, his family offered to assist him with a short-term loan. Had they not done so, BJ's company would not have survived this very difficult period.

Seven years later, BJ's company has become one of the top ten cleaning and food services supply distributors in the Atlantic coast region. The company employs twenty-five people and has a diverse customer base. Its customer base includes an assortment of mid-to-large-size hospital systems, chains of life care facilities, and nursing homes. Having reached a milestone in the development of his business, BJ is now grappling with how to take his company to the next level. Although BJ wants to grow his business, he recognizes he is in a highly competitive market.

Even the most creative business strategy is bound to languish without strong financial leadership. Setting the right course is at least half the battle in achieving Mega Success. Usually, fulfilling the mission requires a solid business plan and a well-crafted financial strategy.

Self-Starters

Are you a self-taught business novice or veteran? You have managed to build a very successful business but secretly continue to struggle with the financial aspects of business management. Could it be that, albeit you enjoy receiving them routinely, your accountant's financial statements have little value to you because you struggle to connect the data in a meaningful way?

Corporate Pros

Are you currently a business decision-maker within a company? Are you assigned the responsibility of managing finances? Under your watch, have profits been sporadic despite exceptional growth in sales revenues? Perhaps under your leadership the company's growth has stalled and lack of access to capital has been a problem. On the other hand, is deciphering the financial jargon that bankers and investors use making it difficult to confidently negotiate a much needed business loan?

Entrepreneur Converts

In your prior career, were you the expert in your field with a well-established business or organization? Now, do you find that you are a novice in managing your own business? Do you feel comfortable with the dynamics of buying, selling, and marketing your business, but feel uncomfortable when it comes to interpreting financial statements, projecting cash flow, and managing profits?

If you identify with any of the profiles highlighted, rest assured you are not alone. Many high-flying achievers have traveled the same road. They endured the same anxiety. For most, the key to overcoming self-doubt was hands-on practice using simple techniques for managing their bottom line. Truth is, if you never learn the process in plain language, you'll always operate in the dark.

Even with a MBA, business experience, and professional guidance, navigating the financial requirements of a business can be gut wrenching.

The flux of financial decisions can be overwhelming at times. Textbook knowledge alone will only carry you so far. Proper direction and orientation, however, will help you gain a real level of confidence.

Most seasoned business leaders agree that navigating the financial perils of a business venture is their greatest challenge. Confusion and lack of understanding the numbers adds even more stress and difficulty. The greatest struggle lies the following: stimulating profit and growing sales simultaneously. To achieve the best results, you have to know how to play the numbers game.

If you are a business leader or hope to become one, *The Road to MegaSuccess* could be the answer to your quandary. Regardless of whether you are new or seasoned, the practical lessons, concepts and real life experiences presented in this book will help accelerate your ascent in the business world. This book offers straightforward guidelines. You may apply these guidelines to profit from and navigate a business of any size in any industry.

My objective is to make aspiring and seasoned entrepreneurs, feel more confident, knowledgeable, and capable of managing the bottom line. By the end of this book, you will be better equipped to meet business challenges with practical knowledge and insight. Let's begin with a conceptual overview of what to expect.

CHAPTER HIGHLIGHTS

- Straight Talk
- Financial Strategy
- Planning for Profit
- Overcoming Roadblocks
- Key Milestones
- Competitive Will Power

A Straighter Pathway

Here's the proverbial "real deal" ... producing healthy profits in any business require three key ingredients.

The three key ingredients are the following:

1) a clearly defined profit strategy,

2) reliable information systems and,

3) strong financial leadership. Of course, this presupposes the business' products or services are marketable and in high demand.

For most entrepreneurs and CEOs of growing businesses, marketing a product to is the least of their worries. Their strengths and talents often lie in sales and marketing. On the other hand, the task that keeps them up at night is figuring how to best promote and sustain profit. Every decision maker faces the difficulty of choosing a route that will most likely result in successful and sustainable profit. If you have similar feelings of uncertainty, do not worry. Help is on the way.

Often, business leaders have a superior ability to devise novel marketing plans and strategically motivate other people. However, secretly many are extremely apprehensive about financial statements, budgets and other tools used to manage and evaluate the bottom line. Here's the good news. Most people can become wise financial leaders with only limited background information about finance and accounting. To get there, you need two things: 1) a thorough understanding of financial fundamentals and 2) a strategic mindset.

Surprisingly, the learning process is tied to as few as a dozen simple concepts. These are more or less common sense principles that underlie most complex financial terminology and applications. Most people are capable of grasping basic accounting applications and tools. However, to improve a business, most leaders will still need some coaching. My goal is to provide the coaching assistance to help you to become a more effective business leader.

......most people can become wise financial leaders with only limited background information about finance and accounting.

We will examine different techniques and approaches for managing the bottom line. However, our main focus will be financial leadership. Effective financial leadership is the all-important game changer. Often, effective financial leadership is the reason why one company of equal size profits more than another company in the same industry. Effective financial leadership is also the reason why one company performs more efficiently than another company.

Let's begin by tackling the root of financial leadership. You'll find that at the root of financial leadership is a well-thought out profit strategy supported by reasonable financial assumptions about the future. The strategy will set forth a plan for managing cash flow, sales and operating expenses. If the plan comes from the CEO, this means his or her grand vision can be translated so that others can study, evaluate, and act on it.

I embrace several basic propositions that I hope you will also embrace. First, in order for any venture to be financially sustainable, it has to generate profit. Second, for any business to run smoothly, financial systems must be developed to track and monitor performance. Keep these precepts in mind. Remember, in order to be successful, you'll need to put certain practices in place to help quickly identify deviations from the plan. Doing so in a timely manner will allow you to take corrective actions if needed. This framework recognizes that even in the best case, a start-up or a growing business will be stretched to the limit. Often, the business' survival will hinge on its leader's ability to navigate the ebbs and flows that come with managing a business.

Financial planning and business management go hand in hand in the business world. Both cover a lot of ground ranging from determining breakeven sales revenues and business financing to pricing strategies. With this in mind, my main focus will be equipping you with the tools to become a proactive leader both in planning and executing financial strategies. It will help you avoid crisis decision-making. By comparison, not only does crisis decision-making leave little room for reflection, it also raises the odds for mistaken judgment. Crises can cause us to become emotional. When emotions are high, rationale can be low. Sound financial planning will help you avoid and navigate crises properly.

To be highly responsive, ready, and able to exercise sound reasoning under fire a business leader has to rely on financial information. Financial information provides business leaders with up-to-date readings on profit, cash flow and any significant fluctuations in the company's net worth. With pertinent data and the help of a quality executive team, the CEO should be able to evaluate the strength or weakness of his or her tactics.

Fairly or unfairly, financial results and outcomes will dictate how others perceive the quality of a business leader's strategies. In turn, it will also be viewed as a measure of his or her leadership ability. Given this significance, I would be remiss not to offer plenty of tips on how to improve your company's financial performance throughout this book. Perception matters.

Pearls of Wisdom

Many people are able to identify with the old adage, "If I knew yesterday what I know today, I would be much further ahead financially." This principle is heard time and again in business. Most of us wish we could get a second chance to apply lessons learned in the past. We also realize opportunities may not always come back around. We simply may not get a second chance. Therefore, the best ways to learn are from others' knowledge and experience and by trial-and-error. Financially speaking, this will keep you out of harm's way. It could help you avoid facing the brink of financial disaster.

The Road to MegaSuccess is designed to serve as a playbook. It's filled with pearls of wisdom. The next chapter focuses on the most common traps that plague growing businesses. Most importantly, it tells you how to avoid them. From the very beginning, a leader will be challenged to make ends meet. Throughout the book, we will use real world examples and chronicle top tier companies in order to illustrate the range of management involved.

In many ways, the insight provided should be quite comforting. For instance, it should relieve you to discover you are not alone in the quest to increase profit and manage your business more efficiently. Even for high-flying superstars, the dynamics of financial management and planning feel perplexing and overwhelming at times. The key to mapping your own roadmap for success may lie in learning more about some of their triumphs and missteps.

You do not need to risk your life savings and personal wealth in order to gain these precious insights. Throughout the book, I offer case studies and tidbits for guidance. Only a few entrepreneurs can afford to ignore templates for success. Most entrepreneurs who use their own money to start a business only have one chance to get the financial leadership process right.

Fortunately, some of the best practices in financial management lay in common life experience. For instance, in real life, people rarely make a major personal investment without doing their homework first. When purchasing a home, most people research the neighborhood, school district, area recreational facilities, and other amenities. The average buyer may go so far as to investigate recent sales of similar homes in the neighborhood. Based on their life experience, they instinctively know many of the best ways to approach the investment and pricing process.

Financial decision-making in business is very similar. Before spending resources to hire new staff, prudence calls for performing a background check. Likewise, before signing on with a major vendor, it may be wise to read its customer reviews. Similarly, before investing in equipment, you will want to closely review the terms and conditions in a manufacturer's warranty. In essence, the reasoning process used in business essentially resembles judgements made in everyday life.

In the business world assessment of the financial pros and cons of a transaction is conveniently referred to as a "cost benefit analysis." This makes the thought process quite simple. It simply entails comparing the potential benefits of a decision against any associated costs. I hope to make you very comfortable using this model and other analytical concepts when deciding when, where, and how to deploy your financial resources.

Without a sound framework an entrepreneur could be tempted to rely on intuition. If so, poor financial decisions are inevitable.

Critical Milestones

Cultivating a strong, profitable business is analogous to running a long marathon. Just like distance runners identify possible turning points in a race in advance, entrepreneurs and other key decision-makers should do the same. Marathon runners contemplate how to keep pace over time. Entrepreneurs should also size up the roadway leading to long-term business success.

A runner spends much of his or her preparation time judging time, distance and landscape of the course. Similarly, using rules of thumb in business is akin to evaluating a long-distance course. Like marathon runners, entrepreneurs must gauge the journey in order to manage their financial resources to win the race.

For business planning it is important to establish financial benchmarks and reference points. This information serves as an alarm system. Whenever there is a major deviation. As the journey progresses, this is the best way to stay on track with respect to operational and financial affairs.

...the entrepreneurial marathon is made up of distinct stages. Each of these stages poses a set of very unique challenges.

The entrepreneurial marathon is made up of distinct stages ranging from wearing many hats to managing your managers. Each of these stages poses a set of very unique challenges both in terms of financial leadership and management.

FIRST LEG

- Form Legal Entity
- Secure Start-Up Funding
- Accelerate Cash Flow and Sales Growth
- Procure adequate Operating Facilities and Equipment
- Implement Transaction Review, Approval and Authorization
- Establish Protocols

SECOND LEG

- Redefine Profit and Tax Planning Objectives
- Upgrade Financial Accounting and Reporting Systems
- Standardize Performance Measures
- Attract Competent Qualified Personnel
- Form Strategic Alliances and Key Business Relationships
- Evaluate Creative Financing Alternatives

THIRD AND FINAL LEG

- Manufacture Profitable Sales Growth
- Build Infrastructure to Support Expansion
- Adopt Risk Management Programs and Practices
- Devise Strategies for Wealth Accumulation
- Implement Exit or Succession Plan

A well-marked roadmap can be invaluable in plotting speed, distance and direction. In business, a map not only helps minimize risk of making a wrong turn, but also assures likelihood of a quick recovery. Based on a concrete set of milestones, entrepreneurs are free to improvise based on points of reference that help calibrate strategies and solutions. Accordingly, each chapter in The Road to MegaSuccess is framed to help you define the most critical milestones along your business journey.

The Power Surge

Along the journey most businesses reach a point where it becomes necessary to secure additional capital to support growth and expansion. In most cases attracting a financing partner—such as a bank or investor—is a prerequisite to long term success.

Financing requirements commonly stem from outlays necessary to modernize technology, attract qualified personnel and purchase operating equipment. Likewise, entrepreneurs commonly look for additional capital to help cover costs associated with rapid customer growth which normally means more capacity. A surge in growth can have major consequences with respect to capital needs and requirements.

Most seasoned veterans agree that access to growth capital is a precious and widely sought competitive advantage. Capital can breathe life into a fledging business and enable a thriving company to reach its full potential. In terms of growth CEOs serve their companies best by forecasting and preparing in advance. Growth capital provides means to increase profits while maintaining quality of service and product.

Many entrepreneurs spend an enormous amount of time and energy attempting to lure capital. However, seasoned executives usually take a strategic approach. First, they study the market to identify financiers that have the greatest potential to be compatible with their business. Next, they work methodically in order to prep their business to pass a series of litmus tests. High achievers recognize the following: if they start planning to look for capital too late, their chances of striking the right deal are virtually nil.

To be a strong advocate and attract prospective financiers, you must understand their lingo. Without some familiarity with the financial jargon bankers, investors, and other stakeholders use, your encounters could be intimidating and confusing. In order to be effective, CEOs and entrepreneurs must train themselves to speak fluently in the area of finance.

While business terms such as net income, profit margin and cash flow differ slightly from common everyday vocabulary, they generally speak to many of everyday ideas. Many of the terms reflect the same concepts we use in everyday life. For instance, before most people purchase an automobile, they pause to assess their personal cash flow. They consider the amount of free cash available each month after they pay their expenses.

Then, they consider that amount of money in relation to the future monthly car payments. They also examine other associated expenses such as interest. Usually, the question becomes how much more will I have to pay in interest over the car's original sticker price? In turn, the seller will most likely run a credit check, ask for verification of employment and examine other information to establish the buyer's good credit.

Now consider a borrower and lender. From the standpoint of borrower and lender, the mechanics of processing a business loan are not materially different than purchasing an automobile. A business borrower will be interested in securing adequate amount of funds to meet their needs at a reasonable cost. Similarly, the prospective lender will want as much assurance as possible that the borrower has the ability to meet their repayment obligations. As you will find later in this book, securing financing is the paramount business negotiation.

Nevertheless, the top priority for most companies is attracting capital. Attracting capital is widely regarded as both a science and an art. The science encompasses understanding technical standards and measures that the lender will use to shed light on the borrower's financial capacity. The art of the deal rests with strategically building relationships and connections that could open doors for financing down the road. The ability to understand these tidbits holds many secrets to profitable growth and expansion. Because the financing process is so important and sometimes elusive, we will cover it extensively in this book.

Navigating the Numbers

In order to achieve success financially CEOs must develop confidence in their ability to understand and interpret their company's financial data. Many are initially resistant because the presentations are not always user friendly.

To some degree, the CPA profession has contributed to widespread fear and trepidation over the numbers presented in conventional financial statements. Often anxiety is attributed to the different formats and labels ascribed to various totals and subtotals. Financial statement terminology is foreign and unfamiliar to most people. Even for those with some proficiency in analyzing financial data, frustration ensues when the desired information is buried and difficult to locate.

The key to better understanding and interpretation of financial information is learning the basic concepts. It makes it far easier to navigate the numbers and use financial data to evaluate performance and map strategy with a conceptual foundation.

When it comes to understanding a conventional set of financial statements, each of which will be described later in detail, I recommend concentrating on the big picture. I will breakdown the true meaning and significance of the three most widely used types of financial statements consisting of a balance sheet, income statement and statement of cash flows. Explanations will be presented in laymen's terms and focus only on the aspects most important to grasp. You will probably pleasantly surprise yourself. I predict you will come away wondering how you ever allowed yourself to be so confused.

Besides technical applications a CEO must have the knowledge and skills to analyze financial statements in order to be on equal footing with investors and other financiers. With this in mind, I want to help you learn to how to confidently assess financial performance and refer to analysis to make your business decisions. CEOs, managers, and entrepreneurs are often bombarded with a constant onslaught of complex questions and emerging developments. As such, they cannot afford to ignore the practical applications of financial statements. More importantly, they cannot overlook the valuable information financial statements contain.

...the art of the deal rests with strategically building relationships and connections that could open doors for financing down the road.

In addition to conventional financial reporting, I will focus on a handful of techniques for monitoring profitability and cash flow. Understanding these models could hold the key to success in managing your business. I assure you that their applications will help you to establish appropriate financial targets. These targets may include breaking even in sales revenues or defining your financing requirements. In the end, I want to enable you to make wiser, more beneficial financial decisions.

Rarely does a business achieve profits on a consistent basis by happenstance. A well thought-out financial plan is mission critical. For instance, no well-meaning business executive would be inclined to authorize purchase of equipment, approve funding for bonuses or sign a contract to purchase commercial real estate, without first checking the budget. Likewise, it would be disastrous to enter a sales contract that did not potentially generate more income than cost.

Entrepreneurs and CEOs alike discover quickly—especially in fast-growing companies—that it is virtually impossible to keep track financially unless you are able to rely on a system that provides a thorough understanding of what is really going on. There is just no substitute for reliable information and analysis when it comes to business finances. As the ultimate decision-maker, your command and understanding of your company's challenges and opportunities could decide whether it flourishes or falters.

The End Game

As a financial leader of a company your role is to be an effective major league coach. By analogy, successful coaching at this level is largely a function of superior scouting, selective recruiting, creative strategy and the ability to make real time adjustments. A good coach also is very adept at preparing their team to compete at a high level on a consistent basis. In similar fashion, a strong CEO relies on validated forecasting, systematic coordination and precise execution to make their company profitable.

In coaching, guiding a team to victory is made easier with a highly choreographed offensive and defensive system. From evaluating competition, selecting personnel, mapping strategy, to play calling sound judgement is called for. A business leader is tested in much the same way. Ultimately, success or failure rests on the quality of a multitude of small and large far-reaching decisions.

As with coaches who have a history of winning there is a high premium on CEOs who have the ability to edge out profits on a consistent basis despite adversity. The job requires smoothing out those inevitable bumps along the road to win the game. In order to complete the mission CEOs must be skillful at devising a strategy capable of surviving rugged tests in competitive situations.

In practice, a financial plan is equivalent to a CEO's playbook. It serves as a pathway for achieving success. It should not act as a set of handcuffs, but as a set of fluid guidelines. It should take into account possible employee turnover, market shifts, financing shortfalls, regulatory changes as well as other potential market changes.

In The Road to MegaSuccess, I will speak about effective financial planning strategies that work in best and worst case situations. Undoubtedly, almost every industry and business must be poised to endure the economy's up and down cycles. The key to survival is a well-defined system aimed at enriching the bottom line.

The key to success is a well-defined financial strategy aimed to enrich the bottom line under both best and worst case circumstances

We will illustrate some of the fundamental best practices for elevating profitability and smoothing cash flow. Before addressing these and other important topics, the next chapter will highlight important personal financial planning decisions and strategies that will help you keep your household enterprise. It starts at home.

NOTABLE REFLECTIONS AT A GLANCE

- Building a financially viable business is not about finding shortcuts.
- Life lessons offer a wealth of guidance on how to manage a profitable business.
- Profitable operations require a holistic financial strategy and strong support system.
- Growth financing follows successful business development
- Navigating financial statements should be as much a conceptual as a detail exercise.
- A mark of good business coaching is winning in the face of adversity.

CHAPTER THREE

Avoid the Classic Pitfalls... Evade the Fault Line

| *The Journey* |

BJ Armstrong reconnects with his former college classmate, Taylor Made, at their 10-year class reunion. The old friends discover they are both entrepreneurs and find themselves trading experiences of business ownership.

Even in college both BJ and Taylor dreamed of owning their own businesses. Straight out of school Taylor accepted a position with a technology consulting company. Five years ago, she launched her own company, Potomac Technologies.

Potomac provides enterprise software development, IT consulting and technical oversight to businesses and government agencies. Its customized software consists primarily of inventory management, distribution, and data processing applications.

After overcoming three years of anemic sales growth, Potomac's annual volume peaked at $5 million and has been flat for the past two years. In addition, the company's profits have declined steadily. Taylor has been struggling to pinpoint the reasons for the change of fortune.

Looking forward, Taylor expects increased competitive pressure as hardware manufacturers increasingly enter the enterprise solutions market. In fact, she is worried about losing two major accounts to large, international competitors. Taylor shares her anxieties and seeks BJ's advice.

Knowing how to promote a business financially requires understanding of the types of classic mistakes that have commonly caused businesses to shut their doors. Sadly, in many instances these business failures may have been avoidable.

For new businesses the highest risk of failure is within the first four years of operations.1 Conversely, while not always worried about failure per se, established companies confront the threat of financial decline well into maturity.

Entrepreneurs in newly minted businesses have to quickly climb the learning curve in order to avoid becoming another start-up business fatality. The difficulty posed for a leader under these circumstances is the necessity to learn while on the job with only a scarcity of time.

Most entrepreneurs are stretched thin between fine tuning selling tactics, marketing, juggling funds, hiring staff and supervising production. In practice, very little time or energy is left at the end of the day for financial planning, oversight and strategic evaluation.

From the start, managing the bottom line in the early stage of the development of a business can be severely hampered due to lack of capital. While financiers have a hefty appetite for growing companies, sources of funding are practically nonexistent for start-up ventures especially while they are struggling to make a profit. The journey from survival to stability to prosperity poses a unique set of challenges and threats at each stage.

For companies that reach puberty and beyond their greatest hurdle is to produce a profit on a consistent basis. To the surprise of many obstacles are formidable. A new business must contend with intense competition, escalating expenses, evolving regulations, and occasional turnover in work force. While struggling through these difficulties a young company also has to devise strategies for boosting cash flow and profits. These are among the most critical daunting tasks every business leader must assume.

As the CEO of a company you serve as the chief financial strategist. Ultimately you must take charge and direct a multitude of activities that have the potential to affect the bottom line. Like it or not, accolades for success or criticism for failure will fall on your shoulders. It is imperative to gain a command of how to make, track and manage inbound and outbound money flow for the odds to be in your favor.

Regardless of seniority, size or industry the secret to enriching the bottom line for any business will involve a combination of interlocking strategies ranging from financial, operational and strategic, to sales, marketing and business development. In this chapter, the most pivotal and serious obstacles that must be overcome from a management perspective to minimize risks of business failure and financial decline will be highlighted.

CHAPTER HIGHLIGHTS

- Financial Missteps
- Uncontrollable Growth
- Cash Shortfalls Deficiency
- Crisis Mode of Operation
- Lack of Financial Oversight
- Apathetic Financial Management
- Misguided Forecasting
- Shake the Mirage

Managing the financial affairs of a business can be very similar to riding a roller coaster – sharp twists and turns at neck-breaking speed. To endure the daily ride, you must have a systematic approach that both measures and manages the flow of resources. This is not only a key to making money in business but to building wealth through business ownership.

Without a solid financial performance monitoring system, most businesses would operate in a grandiose illusion of profit. Often time, dollars hurry in but at a slow rate too slow to keep pace with payment of associated expenses. Likewise, cash flow may be positive one moment and then rapidly deteriorate after payment of a major unanticipated expense.

As most people in business quickly learn, cash in the bank can be extremely deceptive. Cash on deposit is by no means a sign of profitability. You must take into account the entire picture inclusive of pending liabilities and outstanding commitments. Otherwise, it is easy to be misled.

Entrepreneurs are not the only ones at the risk of being misguided about the financial health of a business. Bankers and investors fear making a bad choice of investment based on faulty or incomplete financial information. This occurs most notably in situations where a business owner does not provide a reliable report concerning a company's financial standing.

Sometimes businesses with the potential to become lucrative ventures fail to secure necessary capital simply because their financial information is not readily available. An inability to produce your financial statements is viewed as a trouble sign. When there is no clearly documented trail a small leak in the financial fabric could reach crisis proportion without notice.

It is hardly a surprise that highly successful companies rely heavily on information and various warning systems to navigate through difficult economic times. In essence they carry a toolbox filled with reports that highlight the most critical indicators. Investors and bankers recognize that any CEO who does not have a toolbox leaves their company more susceptible to financial upheaval. However, with the right apparatus a leader is more likely to bypass the occasional fault line and steer performance in a positive direction.

Just as a computer network needs a reliable server to collect and dispatch data, a business needs a dependable accounting system to track financial activity. Having the ability to compile and analyze specific financial data in real time is essential for wise decision making. By analogy, when your computer server is malfunctioning there is greater risk your data could be seriously compromised.

Imagine bidding on a major customer contract without accurate cost information. Perhaps you receive flawed data form your accounting department which in turn used to formulate pricing on a major contract. You go back and forth with your accountant in an attempt to nail down accurate information. Soon, frustrations and confusion lead to a decision solely based on gut instinct. At this point a high risk sets in for grave financial missteps.

To avoid routinely finding yourself facing the predicament described-CEOs should be vigilant about the fine tuning of their financial information and accounting processing systems. The reliability of your information systems could make the difference between business success or failure in the long term. Decision makers supporting the CEO are less likely to make smart choices in the absence of reliable and complete financial information. In most cases it is critical to have hard numbers in order to determine whether to pay employee bonuses, purchase new equipment, order merchandise, or extend customer credit. These types of business decisions should not be made on a whim. For optimal results leaders must have access to as many pertinent and quantifiable facts as possible.

Rarely will a bank, investor or creditor extend funding to a business that is unable to provide conventional financial statements. These reports are not only a reflection of the financial standing of a business but also the quality of entrepreneurs' business experience, industry knowledge and profit strategies. Lenders and investors want to use every means to appraise financial judgment and oversight. They will know to a great degree financial statement information dictates a borrower's future ability to comply with future payment and reporting obligations. For these reasons regular financial reporting is an indispensable best practice.

Every established business should have a regimen of financial checks and balances as well. It is imperative to confirm and verify daily cash receipts, purchases, customer collections and other financial transactions as a business expands. It is practically impossible for top brass to inspect each transaction and, therefore, a strong system of internal control is critical. Financial controls should raise a red flag when the possibility arises things may have been mishandled or errors occurred. While most controls consist of routine reviews inspections and cross checks independent CPA audits should never be ruled out. A wide array of financial controls will be discussed in much greater detail later in the book.

Rarely will a bank, investor or creditor extend funding to a business that is unable to provide conventional financial statements.

Crippling Growth

In retrospect, decade old reports of automobiles that revved up without any pressure on the accelerator were quite frightening. These incidents were described as "unattended acceleration." Although the ensuing investigations generally failed to confirm the existence of any structural defects, the label aptly captured the image of a vehicle taking off on its own beyond the control of the operator.

The concept of unattended acceleration could apply to a business that experiences spiraling and uncontrollable sales growth. Unfettered sales growth could have the same effect as an out of control vehicle, namely, placing the business leader helplessly at risk financially.

Many companies, feeling pressure to perform profitably, are tempted to allow sales growth to rev up to a dangerous rate of speed. When this happens the opposite could occur. Conditions could give way to financial losses brought on by accepting too many high-risk unproductive contracts and customer orders, new customers with a questionable credit history, and new personnel who have not been adequately trained. In the final analysis, rapid sales growth can prove to be counterproductive and detrimental financially.

The level of growth can also sometimes be problematic especially when growth exceeds operating capacity. The incidence of equipment breakdowns, computer software crashes, and processing errors could increase exponentially. Similarly, cost of material and labor may begin to skyrocket.

...sales growth can prove to be counterproductive and detrimental financially.

Starbucks, one of the most successful companies of our day, learned the importance of profitable growth the hard way. Starbucks CEO commented in an interview growth became a carcinogen at Starbucks.

> *When you look at growth as a strategy, it becomes somewhat seductive, addictive. But growth should not be – and is not – a strategy; it's a tactic. The primary lesson I've learned over the years is that growth and success can cover up a lot of mistakes. We're going to make more mistakes. But we've learned a great lesson. And as we return the company to growth, it'll be disciplined, profitable growth for the right reasons—a different kind of growth.*[1]

In its first 20 years of operation, Starbucks' success was built on rapid expansion. During that time the company grew from 11 stores initially to almost 16,000 stores worldwide.

When the Great Recession hit, Starbucks store-to-store revenue dropped, operating income fell and profitability plummeted. Gross profit reached a low of 20% of sales, and operating margins fell to a low of 4.9%. [2]

As economic conditions worsened, Starbucks moved quickly, cancelling planned stores and closing underperforming sites. Despite the firm's seemingly unending growth, Starbucks had carefully incorporated termination clauses into their leases and was able to buy out of 600 existing leases at a cost of nearly $2 billion. [3]

Starbucks also changed its business strategy from uncontrolled growth to realigning the company's cost structure, improving operational efficiencies and use of technology, making strategic investments in key initiatives, expanding product lines and focusing on disciplined global store expansion in key markets.

In the first year after adopting its new strategy, Starbucks realized an estimated $600 million in operating cost savings. Gross margins rebounded to 56% of sales,[2] and operating margins grew to 14.8%.[3] Starbucks continued to invest in redesigned stores, innovative coffee machines, digital networks and rewards programs to enhance remaining store revenues, and worldwide net revenue increased by 40% in just three years.

This revenue growth also reflected the company's focus on less capital intensive and less risky alternative distribution methods. The company continued to introduce new products in its company-owned stores, then partnered with grocery stores, drug stores and clubs to sell products in expanded retail channels. Within two years of its introduction, Starbucks VIA ready brew reached sales of $250 million with distribution at 70,000 outlets worldwide.[3]

The focus on strengthening the company's financial health was very successful, despite difficult economic times. Cost cutting measures and carefully considered incremental growth allowed Starbucks to build significant cash reserves. As the economy strengthened, the firm was in a position to expand via acquisition. Starbucks purchased Evolution Fresh, Inc. and Teavana teas in all cash transactions. According to Starbucks executives responsible for Emerging Brands:,

> *"The acquisition of Teavana supports our growth strategy to innovate with new products, enter new categories, and expand into new channels of distribution. Evolution Fresh, La Boulange and now Teavana demonstration how Starbucks will add brands that strengthen our core offering and create a rich ecosystem of experiences with shared values, mutual efficiencies and complementary characteristics, thus forming tangible examples of the success of the Starbucks Blueprint for Growth ..."[4]*

In contrast to Starbuck's experience, harmful growth can occur as a result of self-destructive pricing policies. New business derived strictly based on low prices could create a false illusion of real growth. While razor thin price margins work for high volume businesses, this approach is not suited for all. Low-ball pricing is prone to financial loss especially where costs of labor and material are subject to wide swings and expense fluctuations. In essence, using overly aggressive discount pricing simply to win market share may pose serious financial risks.

Growth fueled on the backs of chronically late paying customers is dangerous. It is a warning sign that the quality of new business is below standard. Likewise, a significant increase of customers with a poor credit profile is also a cautionary sign. This trend not only discounts the value of accounts receivables but consumes more administrative time and expense.

Poor business practices can adversely affect cash flow. Late customer payments usually cause a slow-down and tightening of cash flow. Likewise, chronically late paying customers squeeze profit margins and could force a business to seek to finance receivables just to speed up collections. The more receivables lag the more likely it will become necessary to borrow increasingly while awaiting collection.

Lastly, uncontrolled growth also weakens human resource management systems. When personnel policies and procedures are revised hastily in response to a heavy and unrelenting influx of new employees in new positions and at distant locations, workflow and efficiency may suffer. As employee ranks swell, a drop in worker productivity usually will follow. This is mostly caused by a lack of supervision and guidance. In combinations an abnormally high rate of employee turnover can take a heavy toll on the bottom line as well.

Late customer payments usually cause a slow-down and tightening of cash flow.

As you will later learn, the key to healthy growth is controlling increased volume and building business infrastructure. New business has to be systematically absorbed in order to achieve best results. Later, I will offer some key insights on different techniques in order to profitably manage growth.

Sharpening Your Game

In order to succeed in business a marketable product or service is an absolute necessity. Just as important, is a well-crafted business model. Even the best laid plans have to continually be updated and revised. This is especially true for entrepreneurial companies with relatively limited capital resources. Business plan adjustments must be made constantly. A prolong delay in business remodeling could cause loss of profits or leave an opening for your competitors to win over your customers.

Many businesses live with the perils that a slow reaction time could have on the ability of their company to survive. General contractors are a case in point. They must be adept at making adjustments in real time as may be necessary for each of their various projects and contracts. Quick response mode is essential to perform within budget, otherwise large sums of money could be lost.

A revelation in the eleventh hour that project costs are at risk of exceeding the billable limits under a fixed price contract is not a cherished experience. Emergency fixes might require contract re-generation if possible cuts in labor utilization or material usage. Unless a leader becomes a master estimator and makes provisions for a reserve for contingencies there is a real possibility of going bust financially.

Unless a leader becomes a master estimator and makes provisions for a reserve for contingencies there is a real possibility of going bust financially.

A case involving a contractor who failed to properly estimate costs and delayed in taking corrective measures arose early on in my private practice.

> *A start-up personnel staffing company began to experience severe financial difficulties even though it had landed a large contract with the State. It never seemed to have enough cash to pay its bills.*
>
> *Even with a potential yearly billing base of $5 million, business debts continued to mount, and the firm began to hemorrhage badly. Average bank balances declined and overdue accounts payables increased. Even when the State agreed to accelerate payment from 30 to 15 days, cash was insufficient to pay outstanding bills. To add fuel to the fire, the company fell behind in payroll tax deposits by more than $150,000.*
>
> *A detailed analysis of direct labor and overhead costs revealed the pricing structure of the contract was ill-fitted. Under the best conditions, it actually would have cost $5.5 million to fulfill the terms of the deal. Unfortunately, all pertinent administrative labor and related overhead expenses had not been fully factored into the contract price during the bidding process. Consequently, no degree of hard work would overcome the structural loss.*[1]

As illustrated price, cost and payment terms have to be carefully balanced in order for a business to make a profit. Sound pricing policies and methods guard against accepting projects that will assuredly end in financial loss. Sharpening the tools of your game whether it be price, staffing or business process serves to help minimize the prospect of taking on new business but ending up in the red.

Even after remodeling and exercising caution, some businesses still incur short-term financial losses. For example, start-up businesses by nature tend to incur losses during their infancy. While ramping up sales revenues, expenses may outpace income. Hopefully, this imbalance will only persist for a relatively short span of time.

After a company reaches profitability it will continually need to adjust and fine-tune its profit formula to remain competitive and strong. Emerging businesses have to concentrate even more in terms of keeping a sharp business model than mature businesses because their capital cushion is so much less.

Crisis Prevention

Surprisingly, many businesses become more adept at reacting, rather than preventing close calls. Rather than focus on proactive strategies to diminish the number of financial emergencies, they tend to gradually accept a crisis oriented culture as the norm. Serious thoughts about proactive management give way to a reactionary mindset.

...it is difficult for any business to operate smoothly when working funds are below par.

Common examples of crisis mode might be where a company routinely finds itself racing to borrow money just in time to meet payroll. Or, when key suppliers threaten to end your business relationship unless paid in advance or cash on delivery. If these types of situations arise on a regular basis a company may be in the midst of a growing financial crisis.

It is important to attack the genesis of any major financial crisis. Understanding the cause is just as important as devising a solution to put out the fire. Often with small companies, the issue is related to a lack of capital. Suffice it to say, it is difficult for any business to operate smoothly when working funds are below par. In terms of priority, the development of a proactive strategy to secure ample capital or debt financing should be a top priority. Most important, the CEO should not wait to the midnight hour because raising debt funding and capital may take weeks if not months.

Preventive problem solving should be the mode in other areas as well. For instance, entrepreneurs who habitually delay solving operating and financial problems may be penalized. Financiers assume—rightly or wrongly—if corrective measures are routinely delayed to the eleventh hour, chances are very high the business will implode. With a short fuse for inaction financiers generally regard procrastination on the part of a CEO as a major risk factor.

As will be discussed later in the book, earning a financier's confidence is sometimes very difficult even with a compelling business strategy. Creating the impression that pivotal decisions are routinely made on a crises basis will not be helpful. In fact, this will suggest business upheaval could be imminent.

Maintaining Close Watch

With ultimate responsibility for financial performance the CEO can least afford to act laissez-faire when it comes to monitoring the bottom line. Effective oversight entails staying on top of certain key facts and figures in real time as they emerge. Cash balances, accounts receivables, accounts payables and net earnings are among the data that CEO's should always be aware.

While it may not be necessary for a CEO to fully understand every debit and credit, he or she should understand the story the financial statement numbers tell. Otherwise, they may be unable to objectively assess the results of business strategies and tactics. One might be inclined to overestimate or underestimate a company's financial strengths and weaknesses. To no surprise, those who spare themselves a regular review of financial statements often wake up only to find their company highly leveraged and swimming in red ink.

To improve oversight, a CEO may choose to model the business to allow for some degree of delegation. Oftentimes, to keep a firm grip operations will be grouped or classified into mini businesses or distinct profit units. These are interchangeably referred to as divisions or departments. These units can be operated like entrepreneurial businesses.

A true profit center will be responsible for preparing and managing a budget. This places the onus on managers within the division for spotlighting adverse financial conditions and taking corrective action. From a CEO perspective, a profit center structure could also help keep the performance of each separate department or division within a company in plain view. It may also serve to promote a healthy degree of internal competition.

Understanding events that affect inflows and outflows of resources on a company wide basis will take in-depth analysis. Shorthand methods normally will not suffice. For instance, rarely can you simply rely on monthly bank statements to gauge a drop off in cash flow. Bank statements are not designed to provide a panoramic view of a company's overall financial conditions.

For purposes of deciphering cash flow, an analytical review of accounts receivables might be necessary. Could the reason for a cash flow decline be that a disproportionate level of customer receivables may have shifted from 30 to 60 days due to 90 to 120 days due? These insights will only surface from a closer inspection of specific receivables within your customer base.

Entrepreneurs and management executives should actively monitor the financial well-being of their business. Experienced leaders quickly come to realize this takes far more than guess work. Intuitively, you may be tempted to believe your company is operating at a profit, however, a detailed statement of revenues and expenses may quickly refute your profitable supposition.

Conscientious managers recognize the necessity to examine and decipher the bottom line. Losing focus of financial conditions could invite early symptoms of financial deterioration. Even worse, by the time problems are noticed the conditions may escalate and become irreversible.

The phrase "work smarter, not harder" has no greater application than in the context of financial management and oversight. An entrepreneur with a growing business will rarely have the luxury of idle time. It is unimaginable to find a leader who is able to scrutinize every piece of financial document and piece of paper. Ultimately, they must rely on well-oiled financial and information systems.

...a detailed statement of revenues and expenses may quickly refute your profitable supposition.

Effective financial management will be a recurring theme throughout The Road to MegaSuccess. To build proficiency in this area, I will closely examine the most common types of financial statements and forecasts, measures and performance drivers.

Self Reflection

Whenever a business leader becomes visibly satisfied with the status quo, it is probably a precursor to financial decline in company performance. Process improvement efforts should never end. If a leader loses the drive to work and motivate others to make things better their company is bound for mediocrity or worse.

When times are good it is very easy to relax and become wedded to a single product, service or customer.

When times are good it is very easy to relax and become wedded to a single product, service or customer. This is especially true when the relationship has been very rewarding financially. During these periods one might ignore the inherent danger in settling on a single source of the revenue for the livelihood of a business.

For many businesses diversification is the key to longevity. Eisner Communications, a 95-year old advertising firm in Baltimore, Maryland, learned this lesson the hard way.

According to reports in the Baltimore Sun, US Airways Group, Inc. was Eisner's most prestigious client and accounted for a sizable portion of its annual income. Advertising Age reported US Airways comprised 40 percent of Eisner's revenues. When US Airways merged with America West, it no longer needed a separate advertising firm and ended the relationship less than a year later.[2]

As reported in the Sun, despite several large clients and frantic efforts to attract new clients, Eisner could not recover from the loss of US Airways' business. The firm limped along for another year and then Eisner closed its doors.

Every company should strive to avoid excessive sales concentration with a single customer or industry. Multiple products, services and customers are a standard for self-preservation. Otherwise, as illustrated too much dependence on a single source of business could be a death knell.

High Definition Monitoring

The greatest mistake some leaders make lies in the old adage, "failure to see the forest for the trees." The lesson of the cliché is of course, a CEO should not allow themselves to become so fixated on one part of the business that other components essential for profit making are overlooked. The financial side of the house, albeit less glamorous at times than sales and marketing, should never be ignored.

Often the missing link in producing sustainable profits a financial analysis under a projection of best and worst case conditions. Advance preparation for things that may go askew can provide for quick recovery if not averting the situation completely. Advance planning also allows strategies and actions to be tested and simulated. Business planning is a treasured opportunity to collect the best minds and devise practical solutions.

As suggested most business veterans classify business plans succinctly into three categories, namely, the best, worst and most likely case scenarios. Business plans that use these points of reference are more practical and valuable. They each present a roadmap for success under the most conceivable set of circumstances.

A select group of powerful planning and diagnostic tools will be on display throughout this book. Moreover, I hope they serve to elevate your financial management skills and ability. The financial models and tools which will be introduced should help improve business planning technique and result in higher profit.

I will cover the mechanics of financial forecasting. No definitive plan should not be implemented without first completing a financial forecast. A well-documented financial forecast translates the owner's future vision and quantifies the expected outcome.

At worst, financial forecasts are good faith estimates and at best, they can be trusted a guide for profitable performance. Experienced business people think of a financial forecast as a roadmap – a detailed outline of performance milestones. It represents a collage of assessments and estimates, linked in logical order and covering a designated time period. Although key assumptions about sales revenues and expenses in these forecasts may ultimately deviate, a solid set of benchmarks increases chances for a successful journey.

In depth strategic financial planning underlies the success of many highly profitable companies. Rarely do major companies decide, for example, to acquire and dispose of operating divisions, roll out product and service lines, or abruptly hire new personnel out of reflex. To the contrary, usually these decisions have these decisions have usually been evaluated and arrived at far in advance.

Should proven financial management techniques that work well for major companies be any less productive when used in an entrepreneurial business? The unequivocal answer to the rhetorical question is, no. Except for scale there are no real discernible differences between big business and small business when it comes to crafting profit strategy or plan of action. The fundamental planning process is all the same.

To embrace best practices, a CEO should develop the mindset and stamina of a marathon runner. The grind will no doubt require constantly plotting time, distance, and position in the pack. Like a runner, to protect his or her advantage, a CEO must strategically exert energy and control their running speed. Leaders must also look to draw from the best models on the market to help build their own financial strength and resiliency.

Before exploring best practices in depth in the next chapter, examine the warning signs in the checklist below to determine if your company could be in danger of falling into the pitfalls discussed in this chapter.

Classic Pitfalls—Early Warning Signs

1. Profits are decreasing, although sales are increasing.
2. Your company is operating in the red, despite having achieved sales goals.
3. Sufficient cash is never available to meet expenses, despite growth in sales and new accounts.
4. Banks, investors, and other prospective financial partners willingly discuss your financing needs, but are reluctant to invest in your company.
5. Your written business plan garners positive feedback, while your financial assumptions and forecasts receive negative reviews.
6. Incomplete financial documentation detracts from otherwise accurate, reliable, and complete information.
7. The legal structure of your business is questioned routinely by third parties for lack of adequacy and consistency with your business strategy and investor relations.
8. The magnitude of income tax liabilities and insufficient cash to satisfy these obligations regularly surprise you.

9. You are more reliant on your own short-hand calculations of net income and liquidity than on professionally prepared financial statements and ratios.
10. You doubt your business would have real value to a third party if you were to sell it.

NOTABLE REFLECTIONS AT A GLANCE

- Avoid the classic pitfalls that lead to financial collapse.
- Promote profitability through thoughtful financial planning.
- Monitor financial well-being on a regular basis.
- Strengthen the quality of your financial accounting systems to improve decision-making.
- Refrain from becoming overly reliant on a single product, service or customer.

CHAPTER FOUR

Plot a Positive Cash Flow... Map Distance and Direction

| *The Journey* |

Although Mediclean has been financially stable for several years, BJ Armstrong still vividly remembers when cash was in short supply. During the third year of operations, Mediclean experienced an extended period of negative cash flow from operations. Had it not been for the equity capital he contributed and for a loan provided by a local bank, the company would not have survived. It was not as easy as it sounds, however, because it took BJ several tries to secure the funding.

Because BJ always had a strong relationship with his banker, he expected the bank would approve his initial loan request without hesitation. Sadly, he was mistaken. At that time the economy was sluggish and his company's financial position was a mess, mainly due to the build-up and delinquencies of accounts receivable. Many of Mediclean's customers were more than 90 days overdue.

The bank was not willing to accept BJ's explanation for the company's tenuous financial condition and turned down his first loan request. For several months BJ had to run Mediclean's operations, get the company's receivables under control, and survive with minimal cash. Those were the most stressful months of his career.

> With the help of a professional accountant and the switch to on-line banking, BJ brought his cash cycle under control. He learned to determine and monitor how much cash was available to run his business on a daily basis. Eventually BJ's banker grew confident BJ would use a line of credit responsibly and approved Mediclean's loan request. BJ knows the key to the turnaround of his business will be his attention to managing cash flow.

Great—a prospect you have been chasing for months just asked for your best and final price for a large contract. You sharpen your pencil, but realize you don't have the cash to mobilize the contract if you get the nod. Your challenge on the front end is to cover 45 to 60 days of expenses while awaiting the first contract payment is received.

Virtually every entrepreneur at sometime has a nightmare that their business runs out of cash or is in danger of not meeting bi-weekly payroll? Or thought the business was in the black just because cash was in the bank only to discover every dime is owed to creditors. Most seasoned entrepreneurs will readily identify with these ever present underlying risks of doing business.

Managing cash flow is a critical survival skill that an entrepreneur must master just to stay afloat. Accordingly, this chapter focuses on effective cash flow management practices, techniques and solutions.

CHAPTER HIGHLIGHTS:

- Managing Cash Flow
- Preserving Liquidity
- Tracking Sources and Uses Of Cash
- Understanding Cash Operating Cycles
- Quantifying Cash Requirements

Net Cash Value

Indeed, running out of cash could be a merchant's worst nightmare. Conceivably, a major cash shortfall could lead to an onslaught of lawsuits, eviction, bankruptcy or closure. As a practical matter, an insolvent company is not able to meet its obligations in the ordinary course of business. It could lose its ability to purchase raw material required to assemble product to meet customer orders. There may be a domino effect resulting in delinquent tax payments. These are just a few of the serious financial consequences that could stem from a consistent pattern of negative cash flow.

To the untrained eye a business may appear to be prosperous or even rich, but in reality find itself in a downward spiral and losing cash by the day. From an operating perspective cash strapped businesses are prone to continually struggle to meet their day-to-day need for cash. They may be forced to forego strategic opportunities with great promise simply because the company lacks ample cash to cover preliminary expenses.

Maintaining adequate amount of cash for operations is the first real test of financial vitality. This involves a company's ability to rapidly convert non-cash assets such as customer receivables and inventory into hard cash. Likewise, synchronizing vendor payments and terms with customer collections is another crucial hurdle.

When the esteemed Warren Buffet's evaluates the importance of cash flow his views are described as follows:

> *"...Buffet makes a conscious attempt to identify companies with a good chance of continuing their success 25 years into the future. Buffett talks a lot about looking through the front window and not through the rearview mirror... Buffet peers into the future partly by attempting to calculate the current value of a company's expected future cash flows. It's his way of assessing a company's intrinsic value.*[1]*"*

From an investor's perspective, cash flow is no less than a lifeline. It signals a company's capacity to payout earnings in the form of dividends and still have sufficient funds left over to cover operating costs. In essence, cash flow is a hard core value indicator. It is also a tale-tell sign of intrinsic strength and weakness.

For analytical purposes it is useful to think of cash inflows and outflows in the context of a weighted scale. The objective is to keep the scale in balance, or in the best case, assure that cash inflow is greater than outflow. Maintaining the equilibrium requires meticulous planning and coordination. If you fail to make a good faith effort sporadic cash shortfalls are inevitable.

A negative cash flow is often attributed to a company being underfunded. This

For analytical purposes it is useful to think of cash inflows and outflows in the context of a weighted scale.

occurs when a business does not have enough liquid cash to move up the chain from infancy to adulthood. Starting a business is challenging by itself and doing so without access to sufficient cash will place a company's survival in grave jeopardy.

Even with a reasonable provision of capital the risk of a disabling shortfall in cash is greatest in the early years of a venture. The same concern could arise even in mature businesses. As new products and services are brought online front loaded costs could consume precious cash reserves.

Many factors, both within and outside the control of a business owner, dictate the flow of cash. Most notably, fluctuations in timing of customer billings and terms of vendor credit can make cash flow highly erratic and difficult to predict. Likewise, the unexpected filing of bankruptcy by a major customer can cause company cash flow to hemorrhage. An unanticipated equipment breakdown, major customer dispute or increase in interest rate on a bank loan can exact heavy blows to cash flow as well.

Significant financial decisions should never be made without first considering the cash flow consequences. Decision makers must keep in mind that an ill-timed expenditure could break the bank. For instance, the outright purchase of new equipment, a vehicle, building improvements or funding an advertising campaign has the potential to deplete precious working capital. From this perspective proper timing is sometimes more important than the actual amount of the disbursement.

Business leaders should also know not to make any major commitments of cash without taking into account the expected future cash position. Current year expenditures could limit a company's ability in the future in terms of strategic movements and eligible financing. To cover all bases the cash flow analytical process should entail measuring, forecasting and historically reporting cash flow.

Managing the Flow

Managing cash flow should be a top priority for virtually every business regardless of size or industry. In the short term, unless a business is cash rich, maintaining a positive cash flow sometimes take precedent over profitability especially for early stage and start-up companies. For newborns, the main goal is to have the ability to pay expenses and fund any business initiatives that need time to blossom. During these periods it is especially important to closely monitor activities that produce and conversely deplete financial resources. Your primary focus areas are depicted in the next chart:

Cash Inflows	Cash Outflows
Collections from Customers	Salaries and Wages
Proceeds from Loans	Benefits Costs
Contributions by Owners	Payroll Taxes
Equity Financing from Investors	Production Materials
Property and Equipment Sales	Office Rent
	Business Insurance
	Utilities, including Phones
	Transportation and Travel
	Loan Principal and Interest Payments

Almost every start-up or rapidly growing business will experience the pressure of a shortage of cash. At times an injection of cash from the outside may determine whether a company will survive and prosper. Start-up expenditures for items such as advertising, supplies, security deposits, insurance, equipment, renovations, as well as legal and accounting services could swiftly deplete liquid funds on hand. When these costs arise and have to be paid in advance of sales and collections, bridge funding is crucial.

Once cash flow normalizes most businesses tend to become self-supporting. However up to that point most small companies look to meet their cash requirements mainly from the owner's personal funds. Assuming business succeeds in generating profits, there is a potential for the owner's seed money to be repaid. On the other hand, in business as in life there are no guarantees.

Before seeking outside funding from a bank or investor, a business should carefully evaluate the magnitude of projected cash needs. This may require examining the cash flow impact and behavior of each major expense line item in their financial statements. Monthly operating expenses such as rent and payroll may have to be paid at times different than installment payments associated with equipment leases and business loans.

When starting a new business or expanding an existing one, cash flow may need to be subsidized for several months or years. For some companies, in the normal course of events negative cash flow is reasonably expected. When the imbalance anticipated running a cash flow deficit may not be disconcerting. Nevertheless, financiers will want to be kept fully informed to understand causes and effects.

Before seeking outside funding from a bank or investor, a business should carefully evaluate the magnitude of projected cash needs.

Assessing the adequacy of cash reserves should begin by plotting your company's cash flow DNA with the understanding that no two businesses operate in exactly the same way. Patterns and timing of cash activity is business specific.

By comparison, two businesses – retail operations and government contracting industries – highlight the stark disparity that may exist from one business to the next. The source of cash flow for retail is mostly over the counter sale, an immediate event. In contrast, a government contracting company is usually required to perform work, and periodically submit progress billings. The latter could also be subject to inspection, audit and regulatory approval before receiving payment. The cash flow DNA in these situations will be polar opposite.

The cash flow DNA of research and development companies is different than most. A business heavily engaged in research and development tend to burn cash at a very high rate especially during the product development phase. There is usually a reversal in cash flow for the better after launch of product sales. It is not uncommon for R&D operations to be funded months or years before a product is actually produced and sold. Accordingly, there will be a much greater reliance on outside funding whenever a R&D business is involved.

Understanding the cash flow DNA of a business is critical for purposes of managing day to day operations as well as for raising investor capital. The basic analysis always begins by mapping a timeline from point of sales billings, receiving cash and paying vendors.

Shortfall Avoidance

Suffice it to say, cash flow shortfalls must be avoided whenever possible. To this end, financial decisions should normally not be hurried or impulsive. Costly missteps are more likely to occur and cash flow adversely impacted.

Each day it is wise to make a complete assessment of your overall cash position. This could require updating foreseeable sources and uses of cash based on customer accounts receivables and trade payables. For most companies these are the primary drivers of cash flow.

Developing strategies for maintaining adequate cash funds should be a primary focus of a business plan. The business plans help prompt leaders to set forth specific timelines and evaluate potential financing sources.

Cash flow planning serves as a guide for estimating sources and uses of cash funds. For instance, while loan payments and payroll tax deposits have fixed payment dates, the scheduling of some other expenditures may be driven by management's actions. Clearly, the best point to perform this sort of analysis is before operations for the year shift into full swing.

The following summary is offered as a checklist to identify line items most likely to impact cash flow:

PERSONNEL

- Employee salaries, wages and benefits
- Employee incentives and bonuses
- Outside employee training

OPERATING CASH

- Vendor and supplier credit obligations
- Contractual debt payments
- Business growth and expansion initiatives

CONTINGENCIES

- Rainy day fund for unexpected emergencies
- Reserves to cover insurance deductibles
- Funds to replace aging equipment and facilities

FINANCING

- Short term debts such as lines of credit
- Long term loans such as mortgages

As Dell computers learned, changing market conditions could also have a major impact on cash flow and may lead executives to revamp strategies and tactics.

Dell Inc. has long been known for its unique business model. Originally the company assembled computers on a made to order basis, allowing each customer to get exactly the components he or she wanted. This model also was an extremely effective cash flow management technique. The company was paid for products before, rather than after, final assembly.

Dell grew to be one of the world's largest personal computer vendors, vying with Hewlett Packard and IBM/Lenovo for the top spot each year, and reached revenues of $61.[1] billion and operating expenses of $49.5 billion (81%).1 Despite its strong revenues and positive cash flow from operations, during that year the company experienced a cash flow loss of $1.8 billion as a result of corporate acquisitions to keep up with technology improvements, and share repurchases.[2]

The company could not recover from these investments quickly. The shift in demand away from personal computers to laptops forced Dell to close several desktop manufacturing facilities. Decreasing profitability, the recession and changing consumer preferences led Dell to critically evaluate its business model and costs. The company announced $3 billion of cost savings initiatives designed to reduce material costs, packaging expenses, and employee wages.[1]

The company's historically strong financial position, buoyed by reduced operating and capital costs, enabled Dell to regain a strong cash position in the following years. Cash flow reached $1.5 billion on sales of $61.5 billion for the fiscal year ended February 1, 2011. At this time, Dell had $15 billion in cash and investments on hand.[3]

As the market continued to change focus, from laptops to tablets and away from consumers to business customers, Dell was able to use its assets to acquire market expertise and share by purchasing software, hardware, service and enterprise solution companies. Specifically, Dell's purchase of firms included Perot Systems, Quest Software, Wyse Technology, Make Technology, Clerity Solutions and SonicWALL, Inc. [4]

While striving to eliminate duplicate efforts and assets, Dell continued its cost cutting measures as it integrated newly acquired companies into its existing business units.

"We are committed to this transformation as we have experienced its benefits. We seek to balance revenue growth with an appropriate level of profitability. In addition, we will continue to manage our businesses to grow operating income and cash flows over the long-term. We believe our strategy will benefit our customers, drive greater efficiency and productivity, and create value for our shareholders."[3]

Plugging The Leaks

Embrace the notion that the management of cash is an ongoing progress that should always be on their radar. Because so many events that occur on a daily basis could be unpredictable no company can afford not to treat it casually.

Even with sophisticated processes and diligent efforts rarely will the timing of cash disbursements and receipts match up perfectly. Even coming close to alignment would feel like Utopia for most entrepreneurs. Sound policy and practice calls for incremental improvements in aggregate to help make the cash operating cycle more efficient.

A graphical depiction of the cash flow cycle in what might be considered perfect alignment versus imperfect alignment is shown below:

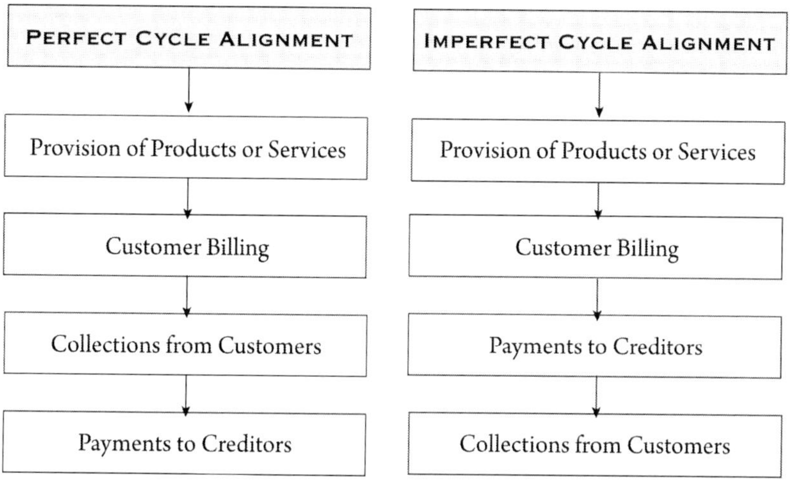

Unfortunately, very few businesses enjoy the luxury of a perfect cycle alignment with that said, tweaking financial policies and practices in order to achieve tighter cash flow alignment should be an ongoing process. For instance, rather than bill or invoice customers bi-monthly consider weekly invoicing. Likewise, as opposed to adhoc purchasing, delay inventory and supply purchases nearer to actual usage. Each of these tactics has the potential to tighten the operating cycle.

Exercising sound discretion in setting customer payment terms is another powerful cash lever. Management is wise to scrutinize standard customer billing and credit policies on a regular basis and make appropriate modifications. For example, to the extent customer accounts can be converted faster from billing to collection, payment in advance or progress payments, the length of the normal operating cycle should be shortened. In essence, payment terms should be tailored to speed the flow of collections whenever possible.

Even relatively minor changes in contract terms stand to yield significant benefits toward a positive cash flow. First, lenders often give borrowers the opportunity to select monthly payment due dates for bank loans and other debts. Choosing a date at the beginning, middle or end of the month may have major cash flow implications. Ideally, you will want a payment schedule to be consistent with the time of month when cash collections from customers are at their highest. Synchronizing vendor payments based on the pattern of cash receipt collections helps keep cash flow in the positive.

A thorough study of cash flow DNA may reveal many other opportunities to expedite receipts and remove bottlenecks. Leaks may be identified in the processing of customer orders, material requisitions, payroll, or customer returns and allowances. Charting the processing sequence may help to pinpoint the source of slow turn over. Shortening the normal lag between billings and collections is an overriding objective in any strategy to improve cash efficiency. Business managers must never assume there is no room for improvement. Many pertinent factors are within management control.

Relieving the Pressure

There are different ways to relieve cash flow pressures. Internal and external means of management require equal consideration. As to the latter, all things being equal management should first attempt to raise cash internally. Given the many possible ways to adjust internal policies and practices to improve the timing of cash inflow is the best place to start.

For example, delaying equipment purchases and payment of bonuses, or renegotiating payment terms on debt may relieve stress on cash flow. When cash is in short supply, adjusting billing and collection can also be a solution. Most of the time it will be a combination of actions rather than a single modification that makes a noticeable difference.

Basic strategies aimed to relieve cash flow pressures fall under two basic categories: (1) those that minimize collection float (the period between when you issue and invoice and receive payment); and (2) those that maximize disbursement float (the period between when you incur an expense and when you pay for it). Examples of these techniques are outlined below:

MINIMIZE COLLECTION LAG:

- Tighten customer payment terms, i.e., from 45 to 30 days
- Tighten credit granting by securing Dunn & Bradstreet and other credible credit references
- Strengthen collection procedures for delinquent accounts with reminders and demand letters
- Offer customer incentives such as a 2% discount for early payment
- Improve product quality thus reducing sales returns

MAXIMIZE DISBURSEMENT FLOAT:

- Control timing of inventory purchases to coincide with the timing of actual usage
- Authorize vendor payments no earlier than the due date
- Minimize operating expenses to reduce burden on cash flow
- Search for suppliers who offer more lenient payment terms

CEOs also should be on guard for cash flow inefficiencies that flow from flawed management practices. For example, often due to employment of a skeleton staff companies do not carefully select the employee to be in charge of billings and collections. There is a perception that only minimum administrative skills are needed, when in fact this person is in control of the business lifeline.

Even in large enterprises, lax supervision and oversight of billing and collection functions is an Achilles heel. Deficiencies extend from a lack of formal follow-up procedures regarding delinquent paying customers, delay in circulating customer payment reminders, to unreasonable delay in correcting routine billing errors.

Telltale signs that turbulent cash flow is on the horizon may include the following:

- Customer accounts 60 and 90 days overdue
- Excessive build up in merchandise held in stock for resale
- Growing overdue balances owed to supplies and other creditors
- Payroll and sales tax deposit penalty assessments
- Overdue lease and mortgage payments
- Arrears on bank loan payments

Banking On It

Beyond operational and policy issues cash management calls for making your money work for you at all times. Accordingly a business should concentrate on accelerating the transfer of funds to interest bearing accounts. They should rarely be parked in a non-interest bearing position.

Investing idle funds on deposit maybe another source of cash flow. Investing available funds as soon as possible and for as long as possible could provide an income stream. This objective may be achieved by working with your banker to devise a cash management plan.

Also, entrepreneurs should not overlook the opportunity to inquire about other types of cash management services provided by banks.

It is rare to find a highly successful business that does not take full advantage of their bank's cash management support products. Common cash management support to look for includes:

PROCESSING

Online banking—Access accounts, loans and lines of credit to expedite transfer of funds and bill payment.

Debit cards and deposit-only atm cards—Distinct cards tailored to meet individual business needs, by facilitating electronic payments.

Credit cards—Short-term financing mainly designed to operate as accounts payable carrying relatively high interest.

Lockbox—Lets the bank perform your high-volume deposit processing.

Imaging/CD-Rom Storage—Eliminates the need for canceled check by providing permanent electronic file of all cleared checks.

Automated Clearinghouse (ACH) Payments—Inexpensive way to initiate future dated electronic payments to your vendors; includes direct deposit payroll.

MONITORING

Daily Transaction Log—Shows all transactions cleared the previous day; allows for daily reconciliation.

Zero Balance Accounts—Allows all sub-account balances at one bank to be swept into a master account for investing purposes.

Controlled Disbursements—Daily report of disbursements to be charged to accounts; allows businesses to add funds or remove excess funds as necessary.

INVESTING

Remote Deposit—Scans checks received for deposit as if there was a physical deposit at the bank.

Overnight Sweeps—Investment of available funds each night.

Concentration Account—Automatically concentrates funds available in multiple accounts at multiple banks into lead bank for investment.

SAFEGUARDING

Positive Pay—All checks written on your account first are compared to the file to mitigate the risk of forged checks.

Balance Reporting—Allows you to see available and uncollected balances immediately.

Armored Car Services—Reduce risk associated with employees handling cash.

Free Cash Flow

When all the dust settles, a determination of the expected amount of free cash flow is the most crucial piece of information for decision makers. This feedback dictates whether the proposed down payment or deposit on commercial property and equipment is affordable. It could also decide whether to pay employee bonuses in the current tax year or the next.

Reliably forecasting cash flow is not only a strategic advantage but an absolute necessity. The feedback you receive could lead to a better system for smoothing out peaks and valleys in working capital, quantify the precise amount of outside financing needed, or method for deciding when and how much divided to distribute to investors.

Savvy entrepreneurs and business executives devise cash flow strategies under best and worst case scenarios. Their planning allows companies to prepare and explore financing contingencies ahead of time. To this end, it would not be uncommon for a CEO to insist on a complete cash analysis by day, week and month.

Savvy entrepreneurs and business executives devise cash flow strategies under best and worst case scenarios.

In order to master the art of forecasting, entrepreneurs have to resist the temptation to pass on preparation of a cash flow projection to their accountants. A CEOs' thoughtful insights and expression of intentions are crucial to development of the projection. Crunching numbers is really the easy part of the process and lends itself to delegation. On the other hand, formulating growth, financing and investing assumptions requires direct participation at the executive level. Investors and bankers expect the company's leader to be the primary architect of the projection.

For illustrative purposes, assume Potomac Technologies (one of the companies in the case study) decides to open a "New Division." In connection with this business initiative Potomac decides to prepare a projection to quantify the cash funding requirements for the first two months of operations. The sample analysis might appear as follows:

NEW DIVISION POTOMAC, LLC

CASH FLOW PROJECTION	MONTH 1	MONTH 2
Beginning Cash in Bank	$100,000	$175,550
Loan Proceeds	300,000	0
Cash Collections from Customers	0	75,000
Cash Disbursements	(224,500)	(196,500)
Net Cash Available for Debt Service	$175,500	$54,000

As a manager assigned to oversee New Division, what response would you provide to the following questions?

a. Without a $300,000 loan, would New Division have a positive cash balance at the end of month one?

b. Was the assumed initial $100,000 of cash in bank critical in month two?

c. New Division's customers will be invoiced "30 days net." The average collections will be, 50 percent of customers made timely and 50 percent within 60 days. Assuming sales of $15,000 in month one, in what time period and in what amount should cash collections be projected for months one, two and three?

d. If New Division is obligated to pay 100 percent of its advertising in month one, should the entire annual expense be factored into the cash flow projection in month one or spread evenly over twelve months?

e. By the end of the second month will New Division have enough cash to completely repay the $300,000 loan?

Upon reflection, would you agree with the following statements?

a. A loan of approximately $300,000 will be critical during the first month of operation

b. An initial $100,000 cash in the bank from Potomac is essential for a positive cash position by the end of month two.

c. The projection of cash from customer collections should be spread over the anticipated period of collection. In this case, $150,000 of sales in month one is expected to be received incrementally, 50 percent or $75,000 in month two, and 50 percent or $75,000 in month three.

d. Because advertising is required to be paid in advance, costs should be reflected as an expenditure in month one.

e. New Division will not be in a position to repay the loan of $300,000 in full by the end of the second month.

In practice, a cash flow projection would typically offer more detail than the sample model featured. Among other things, a summary of underlying operating assumptions, itemized line items for cash receipts and expenditures; and the cash flow projection would cover at least twelve months. An outline of the basic preparation mechanics is provided below.

CASH FLOW PROJECTION MECHANICS STEP BY STEP:

1. Estimate monthly sales and associated billings. The estimate should reflect past sales histories, current market assessment, and marketing plans. Document basis for estimates.

2. Estimate average number of days between sales and collections. This should take into account customer payment terms, past payment history, and other pertinent factors. Document assumptions.

3. Convert monthly sales into monthly cash equivalents based on payment assumptions.

4. Budget direct expenses for cost of direct labor and inventory. Direct expenses generally vary with changes in sales revenue. Delineate payment via same month of sale, thirty (30) days or sixty (60) days. Document assumptions.
5. Identify fixed operating expenses payable each month. Document assumptions.
6. Account for cash outlays for start-up costs and investments in plant and equipment. List any special receipts such as proceeds from a loan or sale of equipment.
7. Compute the net cash balance at the end of each month, and transfer this figure forward as beginning cash for the next month.

NOTABLE REFLECTIONS AT A GLANCE

- Efficient management of the operating cycle improves cash flow.
- Controlling the timing of customer collections, vendor disbursements and/or financing is key to effective management of cash flow.
- A cash flow projection diagrams anticipated sources and uses of cash.
- Internal business practices must be cash efficient.
- Tap into your bank's cash management services to maximize returns.
- For emerging and growing businesses, Cash is King!

CHAPTER FIVE

Net Trumps *Gross*... Adopt the Golden Rule

| *The Journey* |

Several days after reuniting with BJ, Taylor contacted a manufacturer of computer accessories to investigate the possibility of Potomac becoming one of its regional product distributors to commercial users. She believes a preferential marketing and distribution arrangement for computer products such as mice, keyboards, and number pads could be a highly profitable undertaking. Conceivably, Potomac would be in position to achieve two of its main business objectives: diversification and growth. However, such a deal would most likely require Potomac to invest in expanded facilities and hire more people.

Taylor mentioned the distribution opportunity to her sales manager, Eileen Jones. They spent an afternoon pondering its sales potential but were unable to reach a decision. Taylor fears competition would be too strong to generate enough sales to make a profit. In the end they were left with a fundamental unanswered question, what level of sales will it take to breakeven?

Congratulations, entrepreneur! You have launched a highly successful marketing campaign and sales are increasing. Your business is on its way to meeting current financial objectives.

Or is it?

Can it be sales are increasing but profits are decreasing? Is a seemingly lucrative deal about to bring you to the brink of financial disaster? Are you questioning whether a new business product or service will make money? Are you staying up late at night debating whether your business will end the year in the black or in the red?

Profit—or the lack of it—goes directly to the heart and soul of any business. In the long term, profit is the key to survival. In order to be self-supportive your business must have a viable profit model.

Ideally, your profit strategy should insure your company will show profit margin on virtually every sale. In essence, the underlying formula should generate more money from the sale of a widget than it will cost to produce.

A sound profit strategy should yield "net income" once cost of the product and other operating expenses are paid. If you are among the innumerable entrepreneurs and managers struggling to profitably manage the bottom line, this chapter is a must-read.

CHAPTER HIGHLIGHTS:

- Breaking Even
- Profit Modeling
- Planning for Profit
- Strategic Pricing

Conquering "Break Even"

Determining breakeven performance will provide answers to many strategic business questions. Should your company execute or pass up a commercial contract? Could prices be raised or lowered without sacrificing earnings? What level of sales will it take to increase earnings by 10%, 15%, or 20%? Answers to these questions are vital to effective profit management and growth.

The critical threshold for dollar sales of products and services is the breakeven point. At breakeven revenues from sales match operating expenses. Any revenue in excess of this threshold will contribute to what is interchangeably referred to as net income, profit or earnings.

The critical threshold for dollar sales of products and services is the breakeven point.

Financially speaking it would be unwise for a business to sell a product or service below cost except for promotional reasons. Otherwise, with each additional sale a business will lose an increasing amount of money.

Envision the inverse pricing structure shown below:

Sales Price per Unit	$30
Cost per Unit	32
Negative Profit Margin per Unit	($2)

Obviously, it would be counterproductive to promote a product or service that does not have the potential to generate a profit margin. In the example above the product would essentially lose $2 on each sale even before considering basic operating and administrative expenses.

Breakeven straightforwardly asks: How much product or service do I have to sell to cover expected operating expenses? The success or failure of a business venture will depend on both knowing and reaching the breakeven point.

Solving for breakeven requires several steps. First, business expenses have to be classified either as direct or indirect. The distinction between direct and indirect is a function of whether the specific expense involved increases or decreases whenever sales volume rises and falls. Those expenses that fluctuate with sales activity are generally grouped as direct expenses. For most companies, labor and material make up the lion's share of direct expenses.

Expenses that behave different in a more static sense than direct expenses are simply classified as indirect. Characteristically indirect or fixed expenses remain mostly flat even while sales levels rise and fall. Most often items such as officers' compensation, administrative salaries, insurance, office rent, supplies, travel, and other costs necessary to support production or delivery of services fall in this category. The importance of distinguishing direct and indirect expenses will become more evident as we explore several applications of the breakeven model.

For practical context, assume the mythical Potomac Technologies is faced with the following dilemma:

For Potomac Technologies to sign on as a wholesale distributor of computer accessories the company will need to take on additional fixed expenses—administrative salaries, office rent, utilities, travel, and professional and other indirect expenses totaling $425,000. Potomac's direct cost per unit will average $20. The average suggested retail selling price of the accessories is $30. Under this pricing and cost model, what is Taylor's breakeven point measured in the number of units and sales dollars?

FIGURING BREAKEVEN

1. Breakeven Units:
   - Net Profit = Sales Price – Direct Expense
   - Breakeven Point (Units) = Indirect Expenses ÷ Net Profit
2. Breakeven Sales:
   - Net Profit % = Net Profit ÷ Sales Price
   - Breakeven Point (Sales Dollars) = Indirect Expenses ÷ Net Profit %

Based on the analysis highlighted Potomac's prospective new opportunity will not be financially viable until unit sales reach 42,500 units. In essence, it will take selling this minimum number of units in order to achieve breakeven. For decision makers it is critically important to know that until business cracks this sales level it will operate in the red.

A Customizable Solution

By now, it should be clear that calculating your breakeen point is the first major milestone on the road to increasing profitability. Essentially, breakeven pinpoints a specific target benchmark for both sales and expenses. Mastering the technique offers immediate benefit both financially and operationally.

By dissecting the revenue and expense components of your business operation and separating them into a simple equation, it is much easier to formulate a plan to make profit. Furthermore, the breakeven model makes it much simpler to discern whether a new deal, product or investment being considered in isolation offers a realistic prospect of profit.

PRELIMINARY STEP		FINAL STEP	
BREAKEVEN IN UNITS			
Sales Price	$30	Indirect Expense	$425,000
– Direct Expense	– 20	÷ Net Profit	÷ 10
Net Profit	$10	Breakeven Units	42,500
BREAKEVEN SALES DOLLARS			
Net Profit	$10	Indirect Expense	$425,000
÷ Sales Price	÷ 30	÷ Net Profit	÷ 33%
Net Profit %	33%	Breakeven Sales	$1,287,878

Companies express breakeven in different ways depending on line of business. These options include units sold, ticket sales, repeat orders and other quantifiable activities. For example, many service providers, such as consultants, lawyers, accountants, and engineers, compute breakeven based on billable hours. An illustration of breakeven technique found in these businesses is below:

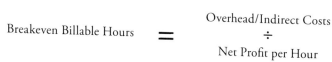

$$\text{Breakeven Billable Hours} = \frac{\text{Overhead/Indirect Costs}}{\text{Net Profit per Hour}}$$

The breakeven model is highly adaptable to practically any business. Several notable specialized industry applications are highlighted below:

- Product and merchandising companies, such as retail and wholesale operations, express breakeven in sales dollars.
- Construction companies typically spread breakeven over a certain number of anticipated construction projects.

- Companies that supply transportation services such as airlines, quantify breakeven based on average daily passengers or passenger miles.
- Healthcare services routinely measure breakeven based on a certain level of patient visits.

The breakeven calculation provides the building blocks for a profitable operation. It serves two distinct purposes: (1) to sufficiently describe management's vision of how the company plans to generate income; and (2) to establish specific financial benchmarks for making money. On the one hand, it is important to remember that the confidence you place in these parameters should be a function of the reliability of key assumptions about each variable and not just the result itself.

The value of breakeven forecasts, largely depends on how well you gauge expected future revenues and operating costs. If the market will not support the assumed sales price, the estimate could be very misleading. To firm up price estimates a market study or survey should be performed.

On the other hand, "tag along expense items" must not be overlooked in estimating direct and indirect expenses. For instance, you will not want to ignore employer taxes, shipping and other expenses that do not ordinarily stand out. The breakeven forecast also should take into account widespread economic changes that may affect the market. In volatile economic times, price adjustments, rate increases, and inflation are likely to occur. Finally, your breakeven should contain a plan A and B, consisting of a best case and worst case scenario.

Even with conservative allowances, a business owner should continually update the projection based on actual experience. In fact, you should assume the targets established will become outdated shortly after a plan has been launched.

Banks and other prospective financiers are keenly interested in management's updated outlook based on their projections. They will want to be informed about the rationale behind revised estimates as well as the underlying facts. This type of feedback can either build or destroy investor confidence. Therefore, your breakeven calculation should be designed to enable a prospective financier to draw their own conclusion about the feasibility of the business model. Even a business' tax advisor will have an interest in financial estimates and details behind the plan to get there.

Finally, in tweaking a breakeven forecast, past experience can also be very helpful. Right or wrong, most outsiders will consider historical financial data as their main reference point when evaluating your financial forecasts.

The Building Blocks

Once your company reaches breakeven, net profit on each additional unit sold should flow right to the bottom line. In order to produce maximum earnings, it is important to specify monthly, quarterly and yearly targets relative to sales, profit margin and expenses. No matter the industry, size, or structure, breakeven planning performed in this manner provides a convenient way to promote greater productivity and profitability.

When deciding how high to set the bar, entrepreneurs frequently ask, "at what level of revenue will the company achieve a profit of X?" To find the answer, the profit or income target has to simply be factored into the breakeven calculation as another component of fixed expense. This allows desired profit to fit neatly into the breakeven equation. Using Potomac's proposed new venture for reference, the following is a chart that would assist Potomac in profit planning:

Alternative Profit Scenarios

Profit Objective	Preliminary Steps		Final Steps	
$100,000	Fixed Expense	$425,000	Combined Total	$ 525,000
	+ Target Profit	$100,000	÷ Net Profit	$ 10
	Combined Total	$525,000		52,500 units
$500,000	Fixed Expense	$425,000	Combined Total	$925,000
	+ Target Profit	$500,000	÷ Net Profit	$ 10
	Combined Total	$925,000		92,500 units

Based on the analysis, Potomac would need to sell at least 52,500 units to generate a net income of $100,000. On the other hand, the company needs to sell 92,500 units to achieve a profit of $500,000. In the real business world, Potomac would also be wise to consider sales demand along with its operating and financing capacity. The latter will be covered in depth later in the book.

Strategically, profit building requires business owners to look to the incremental gain contributed from each additional sale after surpassing breakeven. A grid or step ladder depicting the cumulative gain at various levels may provide necessary guidance for deciding whether to expand and invest in new equipment and facilities. A sample breakdown for Potomac's new venture might appear as follows:

Financial Benchmarks

Unit Sales	-	Break-even Units	=	Units @ Net Profit		Net Income
52,500	-	42,500	=	10,000 @ $10	=	$100,000
62,500	-	42,500	=	20,000 @ $10	=	$200,000
72,500	-	42,500	=	30,000 @ $10	=	$300,000
82,500	-	42,500	=	40,000 @ $10	=	$400,000
92,500	-	42,500	=	50,000 @ $10	=	$500,000

The chart shown above is germane to profit planning. First, it focuses attention on incremental gains based on average profit margin of $10 on each sale. Secondly, it forecasts cumulative net income. Understanding these dynamics is essential when devising a comprehensive business plan.

As a practical matter, breakeven is often used within a company to budget profit between various operating groups and units. It can serve to promote healthy competition within the business. In essence, breakeven may be used to encourage each division or unit to elevate their performance. Finally, breakeven will be a guide for setting benchmarks by product line, region or subsidiary.

Ordinarily, the CEO should have the final say on how to fine tune the breakeven application. Ultimately, they will be accountable for good and bad results. As such, CEOs are either widely acclaimed or severely criticized. With so many estimates involving a high degree of uncertainty decision makers must always be totally engaged and prepared to make real time adjustments.

Improvising to Maximize

At the end of the day, one of the hallmarks of a financially progressive business is an ability to maintain superior financial performance in the face of changing economic circumstances. This may require a high degree of improvisation with respect to price adjustments and cost containment.

A historic look at one of the most profitable privately owned businesses to use breakeven pricing to boost their profitability reveal the secret to the process.

> *Parker Hannifin Corp., a manufacturer of precision-engineered motion and control systems, offers a unique look at how a comprehensive understanding of breakeven can lead to better pricing decisions and greater profitability. As reported in the Wall Street Journal, Parker's CEO eliminated the 89-year-old company's historic pricing policies in favor of "perfect prices." The goal was to use strategic pricing levels to decrease breakeven volumes and increase profitability.*[1]
>
> *Parker produces approximately 800,000 products for clients in a wide array of industries, including aerospace, transportation, power generation and the military. Annual revenues total nearly $15 billion.*[2]
>
> *The company traditionally priced all of its products using the same formula. "Company managers would calculate how much it cost to make and deliver each product and add a flat percentage on top, usually aiming for about 35%." Similar pricing models are used by companies throughout the world.*
>
> *While this pricing approach is relatively simple, it runs the risk of leaving money on the table. It focuses exclusively on cost, but does not take into account the value of Parker's products to its clients. In contrast, strategic pricing emphasizes what customers are willing to pay for products,*
> *taking into account their uniqueness, convenience and competition.*
>
> *Parker divided its products into four categories, from high-volume commodities to highly specialized items. Prices of most commodity products were kept stable, while prices of more unique and customized products were increased. Price increases were as high 60%, with an*

> *average increase of 5%. Even a few prices were decreased.*[1]
>
> *By increasing the prices of items for which the market is least cost sensitive – roughly one-third of the total—Parker decreased the breakeven volume of several product lines. This pricing strategy also enables the company to benefit from manufacturing improvements and efficiencies, rather than foregoing potential earnings.*
>
> *Executives report the strategic pricing initiative has been very successful. Parker's net income increased nearly 1,000% in ten years, despite the effects of the great recession.*

In the Parker case, simple changes in the company's pricing technique did indeed increase profit margins, lower breakeven and thereby yield a handsome boost to the bottom line. Renewed profit strategies often come in the form of more efficient pricing, lowering direct expenses and cutting back on indirect expenses. As suggested earlier, these upgrades must be made continually because the economic landscape of every business and the economy at large is constantly changing.

The CEO's Vision

The CEO's perceptions regarding challenges facing a company, opportunities ahead and financial strategies matter a great deal to all stakeholders including employees and financing partners. The CEO's annual or quarterly message to the company adds credence to company direction and strategic action. As the chief financial strategist others rely on the leader to explain, illustrate and demonstrate the pathway to success in a clear, concise and systematic manner.

A CEO is like a coach with a winning game plan in their head that has to be reduced to a playbook. Every member of the team must be able to comprehend their role and contribution. The playbook should identify targeted sales performance, planned spending, earnings projections as well as any strategic operating parameters. A simple presentation might resemble the matrix illustrated on the following page.

Business Objective	Financial Performance Goal	Time Period		
		Year 1	Year 2	Year 3
Growth	$ Sales	$5,000K	$5,250K	$5,565K
	% of Sales Growth	4%	5%	6%
Margins	Net Profit % of Sales	43%	45%	47%
	Cost Good Sold % of Sales	57%	55%	53%
Financial Return	Net Income	$431K	$450K	$500K
	Net Income % of Sales	9%	9%	9%
Quality Assurance	Purchase Return % of Sales	0.5%	0.5%	0.5%
	Sale Return % of Sales	2%	2%	1%
Human Resources	Salaries % of Sales	12%	13%	14%
	Employee Benefit % of Salaries	20%	20%	20%
Distribution of Earnings	$ Dividend (Earnings) Payout	$100K	$150K	$200K
	Dividends % of Net Income	23%	33%	40%

The CEO's outlook on future financial performance establishes a benchmark for performance. Accordingly, it should be outlined in a framework that when applied will promote the collective work effort. The aim to synchronize marketing campaigns, hiring decisions, equipment purchases, infrastructure, investments and other business activity. The leader's compilation of views and thoughts should leave no doubt or questions in the following areas:

- What is the expected revenue in years one through three?
- What is the profitability target over the next three years?

- What overall profit margin level is necessary for the company to achieve its financial objectives?
- What resources will be acquired and made available to facilitate expected performance?

The opportunity to articulate specific financial goals and success measures should be treasured. It is an opportunity to motivate company personnel. Just as important, this guidance will be the foundation for others to develop processes and policies over sales, production and budgets. Always remember, in the end the most important voice of a company is not its executive Vice President, Business Attorney or CPA, but its CEO.

NOTABLE REFLECTIONS AT A GLANCE

- Breakeven constitutes a barometer for business management.
- Simple profit-modeling estimates direct and indirect expenses in computing margins.
- Breakeven drives development of performance goals and standards.
- Breakeven models must be customized to business and industry.
- Net always trumps Gross.

CHAPTER SIX

Leverage Your Financials... Get a Reality Check

| *The Journey* |

Taylor Made has good news: Potomac is being considered for several large contracts, each of which offers the potential for a handsome financial return. Taylor knows that these potential contracts will require expenditures for additional staff and equipment. Accordingly, Taylor pulls out Potomac's most recent financial statements. In the course of her review, she realizes all the cash in bank is already reserved for other business needs. Potomac needs to pay outstanding supplier invoices. However, once it fully collects money from accounts receivable, Potomac should be able to spare some cash to fund the most important contract expenses.

Taylor was happy to learn about Potomac's income statements from last year. However, her excitement tempered quickly. Taylor learned that in the past two years, there had been no significant increase in sales revenues. Last year, in an attempt to spark sales growth and qualify for large contracts, Taylor authorized purchase of new equipment to enhance the company's operating capacity. Now, she wonders how the investment in equipment will show up on the company's cash flow statement and balance sheet.

> In anticipation of the new contracts, Taylor requested a meeting with Steve Pool: the company's banker. After all, Taylor was anticipating new contracts and cash low. She thought it would be wise to discuss the possible need for short-term funding. Surprisingly, however, Steve requested Taylor supply her company's most recent financial statements in advance of the meeting. Then, panic ensues. Taylor quickly realizes that she will have to discuss Potomac's financial statements with Steve without her accountant present.
>
> Taylor is not the first, nor the last, CEO to find him or herself in this predicament. Remember the adage, "A picture is worth a thousand words?" Financial statements are your business' self-portrait. In the digital sphere, financial statements function as high-resolution pictures or "selfies" without a filter. In the medical sphere, think of them as X-rays. However you remember it, just remember the "picture" of your business that derives from your financial statement is worth a thousand words.

When outsiders evaluate your company's financial status, they will not take your word for it. Rather, they will examine your company's financial statements. Financial statements validate—or invalidate—your business' reliability and completeness. Whether you are attempting to secure a business loan, commercial mortgage, vendor credit, or investor capital, the content and quality of your financial statements is a litmus test. The story they tell has many chapters —including your profitability, assets, debts and equity—just to name a few. Your company's financial statements also indicate the strength of your company's financial infrastructure. From an outsider's perspective a company that lacks the ability to produce financial statements may also lack the capacity to manage funds profitably.

Financial statements benefit your business in two fundamental ways. First, financial statements track the history of financial resources. Second, they provide a way to track financial performance in real-time. Thus, investors, bankers, and other interested third parties look at financial statements to find answers to their questions. As such, financial statements are critical for sound management and performance evaluation.

Do you feel uncomfortable navigating between different financial statements? Do you have difficulty locating critical financial information about your business? Do you feel like Taylor Made felt? That is, overly dependent on your accountant to interpret the meaning of the financial data? Taylor did not experience this yet—but have you ever been shocked by a potential investor's unfavorable conclusions about your company's financial strengths and weaknesses? If you answered yes to any of these questions, this chapter will help. The following chapter speaks to a large chunk of entrepreneurs—especially those that experience anxiety, frustration or confusion interpreting and applying financial statements.

CHAPTER HIGHLIGHTS

- Fundamentals of Financial Statements
- Financial Statement Applications and Uses
- Needs of Investors and Bankers
- Management Guides for Interpretation
- Analytical Insights

Inside the lines

Financial statements play a vital role in fueling company commerce. They are a universally accepted report card used to compare one company to another company. The final grades depend solely on the numbers within the four corners of each page, on top of each line. When assessing a business overall the true story about the financial condition and quality of past performance lies inside the lines. Outsiders derive and collect feedback from financial statements. The feedback derived from a set of financial statements provides a chronology of a company's financial history. It is also an indication of their current financial status.

The phrase "financial statements" normally refers to three conventional report types:

1. Income Statement,
2. Balance Sheet and
3. Cash Flow Statement.

Each report provides quantitative financial information that speaks to a specific area of business up keep and maintenance. Financial statements also collectively offer a snapshot of a company's financial makeup.

The title of each financial statement explains its purpose and application. It helps to think about each financial statement in everyday terms. For instance, CEOs tend to concern themselves with bottom line earnings (income statement), cash generated (cash flow statement) and net worth (balance sheet). I highlight the bare bones of each financial statement below:

Income Statement	Measures profitability—revenues from sales less costs of products or services and any other expenses necessary to operate the business. Normally covers a month, quarter, or year.
Cash Flow Statement	Breakdown of cash activity—lists all sources and uses of cash whether tied to operations, capital infusions or loans. Report captures activity during a month, quarter or year.
Balance Sheet	Addresses liquidity and net changes in worth—reports detailed company assets, liabilities and equity. Pinpoints financial status at the end of a month, quarter or year.

Every business should have a financial health evaluation periodically. Consider what occurs when a patient gets an X-ray. Any spots on the x-tray may reveal abnormalities. Financial statements also highlight unusual patterns. Scrutinized items range from assets, liabilities, capital, revenues and expenses to cash proceeds from assets sales, loans and contributed capital.

Business leaders should not only concern themselves with periodic financial report cards, but also their business' performance or shortcomings. Financial statements are guides for financial planning. Considering the potential insights financial statements offer, a poorly constructed set of financial statements could mislead decision-makers. They could camouflage harsh financial realities.

The type of vital feedback most beneficial for management include the following:

- Decreased profitability due to increased cost of goods sold. The income statement would reflect a reduction in "gross profit." Gross profit is gross sales minus cost of goods sold.

- Tight cash flow due to slower customer payments. The balance sheet could indicate signs of this condition as increased "accounts receivable." The statement of cash flow may reflect a reduction in cash from operations.
- Exceedingly high vendor credit. This problem would be evidenced by higher "accounts payable" on the balance sheet. The cash flow statement would report it as a growing source of financing on the cash flow statement.
- Higher pricing coupled with cuts in expenses. Results of this strategy would reveal itself on the income statement where one would expect net income to increase.
- Financial effects of a rollback in inventory purchasing. The balance sheet should highlight effects in two places: 1) Reduction in inventory and 2) Accounts payable.
- An income statement that reflects financial operating percentages by expense line item and net earnings as a percentage of total sales revenues.
- Loss or retirement of major equipment. Changes in equipment's book value would be reflected both on the balance sheet and the cash flow statement.

It may surprise you to learn that some leaders downplay the value of financial statements. They dismiss their usefulness believing financial statements are no more than abstract information for income tax reporting or for satisfying financiers. However, by doing so they overlook numerous practical applications that could improve the bottom line.

Financial Statements provide answers to many questions raised by management and external parties, especially investors and bankers. Ideally, each person should be able to read into the numbers and determine what they say about the company's past, present and future. Therefore, diminishing the role and applications of financial statements is not an optional move for business owners.

Failing to tap into the power of financial statements would be a big mistake. Consider a doctor who ignores symptoms of disease in a patient. He or she would be regarded as inept in the medical profession. So too, a CEO who ignores or chooses not to take time to develop critical financial information unnecessarily risks his or her company's financial health.

Bird's Eye View

A closer look into the content of each report amplifies the practical uses of each financial statement. Look closely at the chart below. The chart highlights the particular features of the Income Statement, Cash Flow Statement and Balance Sheet.

MANAGERIAL APPLICATIONS OF FINANCIAL STATEMENTS

REPORT TYPE	INCOME STATEMENT	CASH FLOW STATEMENT	BALANCE SHEET
Function	Net income or loss resulting from gross revenues less expenses	Measurement of major inflows and outflows of cash	Increases and decreases in assets, liabilities and equity
Content	Specific revenue and expense line items and cumulative totals for year, quarter or month	Sources and uses of cash and cumulative totals for year, quarter or month	Categorical itemization of assets and liabilities, and balances at specified dates
Bottom Line	Net Income (Loss)	Net Increase (Decrease) in Cash	Net Increase (Decrease) in Equity

A full blown sample financial statements is provided later in this chapter. However, the chart above serves as a quick reference on how to navigate financial statements and answer important questions.

After you grasp a conceptual understanding of how to use financial statements, your next task is to learn the relevant terms. Familiarizing yourself with the lingo adds to your proficiency and enables you to take full advantage of all financial opportunities. I present functional definitions and instructions to help you in the remaining sections of this chapter.

Income Statement Terms

Revenues comprise gross funds received in dollars or amounts owed to the company by customers from the sale of goods and services.

Expenses are the costs fully incurred by the business and typically are divided into costs of goods sold (*items needed to produce a product or service*) and operating expenses (*items such as rent, salaries, insurance and advertising incurred in managing the business*).

Cash Flow Statement Terms

Sources of cash include net income, bank loans, and contributions by owners.

Uses of cash include loan payments, equipment purchases, and technology investments.

Balance Sheet Terms

Assets include the items of value possessed by the company for future benefit. Asset value is generally equal to the lower of the purchase price or market value.

Liabilities consist of legally enforceable financial obligations such as vendor invoices, unpaid taxes and outstanding loans.

Equity is the net dollar difference between the stated values of the company assets and liabilities.

The explanations above also illustrate the logic behind grouping dollars relating to certain activity. Even when these titles vary slightly, in practice their application is the same. Cash flow and balance sheet applications are essentially the same regardless of business type or industry net income.

GAAP Reporting

Conventional financial statements are required to adhere to certain basic accounting standards and methods. The requirement ensures users can interpret and compare financial statements universally. The rules are referred to as Generally Accepted Accounting Principles (GAAP). CPAs are required to observe the guidelines when preparing financial statements or when rendering a professional opinion on them.

For most non-accountants, the most important thing to remember about GAAP is its main purpose: to promote uniformity and consistency in presentation. GAAP provides commonly accepted methods of measuring gains, losses, increases in value and decreases in value. Without it, investors, bankers and business owners could find themselves confused or misled.

One of the first criteria of accounting regulated under GAAP is logging in all cash receipts and disbursements. Another, and perhaps more important class of restrictive guidelines, are those that decide how financial values are measured. Specific criteria ranges from corporate investments, equipment, real estate and liabilities such as mortgages and long-term leases. Other rules span from write downs on items such as delinquent customer receivables to valuation of copyrights, trademarks and intellectual property.

GAAP provides assurance to investors and bankers that companies are playing by the same rules. They enable third parties to compare and contrast performance under a common set of accounting standards. Entrepreneurs should also welcome these guidelines as a means for enhancing the quality of information used for decision-making.

Decision-Making Guidance

Reliable financial statements are key to sound decision-making in business. Consequently, it is customary for financial statements to be prepared on the basis of monthly, quarterly or annual periods. New and expanding companies are especially advised to financially report frequently.

It is easier to spot varying trends in financial condition and direction when they are stacked side-by-side, year-by-year. Results of a management strategy are more evident when examining two or more prior periods as a financial baseline. For this reason, feedback from financial statements is invaluable for most companies.

To improve financial performance, entrepreneurs and key decision-makers should be able to count on financial statements to quantify their financial well-being. Furthermore, lenders and investors rarely accept verbal representations of profitability, liquidity and net worth. Financial statements also serve to keep stakeholders informed and aware of a company's real financial circumstances. Financial statements are the most objective and reliable manner for determining the financial standing of a business within a particular industry.

Although entrepreneurs may direct their accountants to prepare their financial statements, they should never be out of touch with its content or quality. In the end, financial statements will be regarded as management's representations rather than those of their accountants. Quality and completeness are a reflection on management's integrity and competence. In the next chapter, we will review the analytical techniques financers use in depth. For the most part, these methods focus on specific segments of each of three basic financial statements.

In summary, conventional financial statements represent a well-defined system of keeping score of your financial performance and condition. Adherence to GAAP ensures the financial statements of multiple companies are comparable. While the accounting framework provides specific rules for financial reporting valuation, a reasonable amount of flexibility exists.

Hands-On Application

Assume the CEOs of Mediclean, Inc. and Potomac, LLC have arranged to meet with their respective bankers. Mediclean's intention is to secure financing for expansion. Potomac, on the other hand, needs working capital to pursue several potential large contracts. The following pages contain sample income statements, cash flow statements and balance sheets for each company. They are also navigation guides to help you understand the statements presented.

Consider the information you just read. If you were in the banker's shoes, how would you rate their respective financial statements?

INCOME STATEMENT(S)
FOR THE YEAR ENDED DECEMBER 31, 20XX

	MATRIX, INC.	POTOMAC, LLC
REVENUES		
Maintenance Products	$10,500,000	$ —
Hospitality Products	26,000,000	—
On-Line Services		2,750,000
Software Support Services		2,250,000
Total Revenues	36,500,000	5,000,000
COST OF GOODS/SERVICES		
Cost of Goods Sold – Maintenance Products	7,350,000	$ —
Cost of Goods Sold – Hospitality Products	16,900,000	—
Direct Labor – On-Line Services		1,512,500
Direct Labor – Software Support Services		1,350,000
Total Direct Expenses	24,250,000	2,862,500
Gross Profits	12,250,000	2,137,500
DIRECT SELLING EXPENSES		
Commissions	1,830,000	—
INDIRECT EXPENSES		
Salaries and Wages (Admin & Mgmt)	2,280,000	550,000
Employer's Payroll Taxes	170,000	50,000
Equipment Leasing	480,000	140,000
Utilities	260,000	100,000
Rent – Warehouses/Office	2,500,000	260,000
Office Expenses	170,000	70,000
Insurance	140,000	50,000
Dues and Licenses	50,000	20,000
Repairs and Maintenance	80,000	40,000
Travel and Transportation	20,000	140,000
Advertising	480,000	80,000
Legal and Accounting	120,000	20,000
Interest	420,000	36,000
Depreciation	170,000	20,000
Total Expenses	9,170,000	1,576,000
Net Income Before Taxes	3,080,000	561,500
Income Tax Expense	(1,250,000)	(130,000)
NET INCOME	$1,830,000	$431,500

The Income Statement Quick Navigation Guide:

Revenues from Sales	Under the Accrual Method of Accounting revenue is reportable at the time of billing not collection. Includes revenues from products and services, as appropriate.
Less Cost of Sales	Costs of services rendered and products actually sold. For products includes merchandise, material, assembly labor and other direct product expenses. For services includes labor, commissions and other direct service costs.
Less Operating Expenses	Under the Accrual Method expenses are recognized when incurred, not time of payment. Includes owners' and managers' salaries, office rent, insurance, advertising and other operating expenses.
Equals Net Income or Loss	Profit or loss from operations.

Statement of Cash Flows
For the Year Ended December 31, 20XX

	Matrix	Potomac
Cash Flows from Operating Activities		
Net Income from operations	$1,830,000	$431,500
Adjustments:		
Depreciation	170,000	20,000
Increase in Accounts Receivable	(100,000)	(100,000)
Increase in Merchandise Inventory	(500,000)	
Increase in Accounts Payable	250,000	(100,000)
Decrease in Sales Taxes Payable	(50,000)	
Increase in Payroll Taxes Payable	20,000	(50,000)
Net Cash Provided by Operating Activities	1,620,000	201,500
Cash Flows from Investing Activities		
Purchase of Equipment/Furnishings	(800,000)	(126,000)
Purchase of Real Estate	(200,000)	
Net Cash Used in Investing Activities	(1,000,000)	(126,000)
Cash Flows from Financing Activities		
Loans – Repayment of Principal	(520,000)	(50,500)
Net Cash Used in Financing Activities	(520,000)	(50,500)
Net Increase in Cash	100,000	25,000
Cash in Banks, Beginning of Year	320,000	60,000
Cash in Banks, End of Year	$420,000	$85,000

Statement of Cash Flow Quick Navigation Guide:

Sources of Cash	Cash inflows from all sources are identified and taken into account. Typically they include: • Net Cash from Operations (i.e. collections from sales less expenses paid) • Proceeds from Bank Loan • Contribution of Capital by Owners • Proceeds from Owners' Loan to Company • Other Sources of Cash
Less Uses of Cash	Outflows other than normal operating expenses are designated and reported. Typically, these items consist of the following: • Loans—Payments • Purchase of Equipment • Purchase of Real Estate • Other Cash Outflows
Equals Net Increase or Decrease in Cash	Represents the difference overall.

BALANCE SHEET
DECEMBER 31, 20XX

	MATRIX	POTOMAC
ASSETS		
Current Assets		
Cash in Banks	$420,000	$85,000
Accounts Receivable – Trade	1,500,000	240,000
Merchandise Inventory	2,420,000	--
Total Current Assets	4,320,000	325,000
Non-Current Assets		
Loans Receivable – Employees	25,000	25,000
Security Deposits	50,000	30,000
Equipment/Furnishings (Net of Accumulated Depreciation)	1,700,000	200,000
Investment in Real Estate	1,000,000	--
Total Non-Current Assets	2,775,000	255,000
TOTAL ASSETS	7,115,000	580,000
LIABILITIES		
Current Liabilities		
Accounts Payable – Trade	1,850,000	85,000
Sales Tax Payable	150,000	--
Payroll Taxes Payable	40,000	15,000
Loan Payable Bank – Current	420,000	50,000
Total Current Liabilities	2,460,000	150,000
Long Term Liabilities		
Loan Payable Bank – Long Term	1,780,000	250,000
Loans Payable – Officers and Shareholders	150,000	30,000
Total Long Term Liabilities	1,930,000	280,000
TOTAL LIABILITIES	4,390,000	430,000
EQUITY		
Common Stock/Member Capital	2,000,000	70,000
Retained Earnings/Members' Equity	725,000	80,000
Total Stockholders'/Members' Equity	2,725,000	150,000
TOTAL LIABILITIES AND STOCKHOLDERS'/MEMBER'S EQUITY	$7,115,000	$580,000

Checkpoints for Novices

The profiles of Mediclean and Potomac display the broad range of financial data contained in a basic set of financial statements. If you are a novice or just becoming acquainted with these presentations, you could benefit from walking through the main checkpoints.

The Income Statements for Mediclean and Potomac, reveal the following:

1. Mediclean's gross profit on Dining Room Products exceeds that of its Cleaning Products.

	CLEANING	DINNING ROOM
Revenues	$10,500,000	$26,000,000
Cost of Goods Sold	$7,350,000	$16,900,000
Gross Profit	$3,150,000	$9,100,000

2. Potomac's On-Line Services have a higher margin than the company's Software Support Services.

	ON-LINE	SOFTWARE
Revenues	$2,750,000	$2,250,000
Cost of Goods Sold	$1,512,500	$1,350,000
Gross Profit	$1,237,500	$900,000

3. By comparison, Mediclean's net income is greater than Potomac's net income.

	MEDICLEAN	POTOMAC
Net Income	$1,830,000	$431,500

The illustrative Statements of Cash Flow for each company pinpoint the followin with respect to sources and uses of cash:

1. Mediclean and Potomac each generated positive cash from their respective operations for the year.

	MEDICLEAN	POTOMAC
Net Cash from Operations	$1,620,000	$201,500

2. For Potomac, several key operating factors minimized the amount of cash generated from operations.

Increase (build up) in Accounts Receivable	$100,000
Decrease in (pay down) of Accounts Payable to Vendors	$100,000
Decrease in (pay down) Payroll Taxes	$50,000

3. Mediclean and Potomac each expended cash or financing to purchase long-term assets.

	MEDICLEAN	POTOMAC
Purchase of Equipment/Furnishings	$800,000	$126,000
Purchase of Real Estate	200,000	0
Total Additions	$1,000,000	$126,000

4. Mediclean and Potomac each used their cash to retire long term debt.

	MEDICLEAN	POTOMAC
Repayment of Loan Principal	$520,000	$50,500

A close examination of the Balance Sheet of each company will shows the following:

1. Total assets reported by Mediclean and Potomac respectively:

	MEDICLEAN	POTOMAC
Total Assets	$7,115,000	$580,000

2. The most liquid assets of each company can be found classified under "Current Assets."

	MEDICLEAN	POTOMAC
Cash In Banks	$420,000	$ 85,000
Accounts Receivable	1,500,000	240,000
Merchandise Inventory	2,420,000	0
Total Current Assets	$4,340,000	$325,000

3. Total liabilities having a maturity (payment due date) of one year or less are classified under the heading of "Current Liabilities".

	MEDICLEAN	POTOMAC
Total Current Liabilities	$2,460,000	$150,000

NOTABLE REFLECTIONS AT A GLANCE

- Conventional financial statements consist of the Income Statement, Cash Flow Statement and Balance Sheet
- Conventional financial statements document financial activity holistically.
- Regular financial statement review and analysis serves to improve overall financial performance.
- Reliable and accurate financial statements are essential for strategic planning and business valuation.
- Investors and bankers rely on financial statements, not words.
- An ability to interpret financial statements is one key to managing growth, costs and profitability.

CHAPTER SEVEN

Monetize the Enterprise... Build Economic Stamina

| *The Journey* |

BJ and Taylor continue to meet regularly to reflect on their respective business aspirations, challenges and opportunities. Even though Mediclean has been relatively successful financially, the company has areas of weakness that have become quite visible under close scrutiny.

Under close scrutiny Mediclean appeared to be losing steam financially. The banker noticed that Mediclean's inventory turnover ratio was decreasing; indicating inventory may not be moving off the shelves as quickly as it did in the past. Likewise, the average days' sales in accounts receivable had climbed upward suggesting customer collections have slowed in proportion to sales revenue.

BJ invited Taylor to chime in on the banker's comment, and the friends discussed possible reasons for the fall off. They wondered whether Mediclean was unknowingly overstocking certain goods no longer in high demand. The idea also surfaced that Mediclean's customer credit screening may need to be revamped to ensure credit is being granted selectively.

BJ intends to expand the financial analysis into other operating and financial activities. For instance, he would like to

> review fluctuations in ratios and percentages applicable to his cash flow, debt coverage and return on investment. Even though Mediclean obtained additional funding a year ago, he would like to verify that Mediclean is still in compliance with each of the financial covenants of its bank loan. The contract provisions stipulate that certain minimum financial thresholds must be maintained especially in the area of debt coverage.

You are frantic! You just learned that on a cumulative basis your company's current debt exceeds the maximum allowable limit permitted under its bank loan agreement. This is revealed as your most recent financial statements are about to be submitted to your banker to request the loan limit be raised.

Or just as shocking. While investigating the underlying cause for the spike in debt, you discover cash in the bank is much lower than normal. In fact, you review some recent bank statements and find certain unexplained electronic transfers and automatic debits to the account. Other than withdrawals covering your regular monthly bank loan payment, you have no knowledge about these other automatic bank debits or electronic fund transfers.

Just imagine being faced with the proverbial double whammy, uncontrollably rising debt plus possible evidence of theft. How easy these circumstances might arise without an internal alarm system. Financial oversight and management control systems fulfill this purpose. These safeguards are necessary to monitor key financial vital signs.

CHAPTER HIGHLIGHTS:

- Health and Wellness Index
- Vital Percentages and Ratios
- Industry Norms
- Financial Safeguards
- Routine Check-Ups

Health and Wellness

You may ask what constitutes sound financial health and wellness for a business enterprise. The simple answer lies with about a dozens quantifiable and qualitative factors. These markers are mostly tied to profitability, efficiency, and liquidity. Too many decision makers fail to take time to fully understand how to apply and interpret these metrics.

Rarely will a banker or financier rely exclusively on financial statements to judge the health and wellness of a company. Financial statements prepared according to Generally Accepted Accounting Principles (GAAP) are intended to be informative for a general audience. To become comfortable about investing Lenders and Investors need much more.

If you are searching for a major financial investor they should be prepared to provide information that goes deeper than normal. Financiers want detailed feedback and disclosures. Indeed, depending on the amount of funding involved financiers will insist on a complete financial DNA. Their issues and concerns relate to your company's economic stamina or visibility as well as its profitability.

At first glance the financial statements of a company can be deceiving. For instance, a company may show a high sales growth rate but simultaneously sustain a significant decline in net earnings. Likewise, there may be a sudden build up in the balance of uncollectible accounts receivables at a faster rate than growth in new sales. Or, sales growth may be flat but debts skyrocket for no apparent reason. In any of these situations financers will conclude financial trouble maybe imminent for the business.

Among top tier financers it is customary to perform a complete financial inspection of an investee company up front. Investors and bankers commonly refer to this as "due diligence." The process spills over into various financial, operational as well as legal affairs of a company. Knowledge and understanding of conventional practices can be a major advantage when making a pitch for funding.

The Diagnostic Process

The scope of a thorough health evaluation of course will depend on the nature of the business. For instance, assessing a dry cleaner will normally take far less analysis than an engineering or manufacturing firm. As part of the process financiers routinely request independent verification of bank account balances, make in depth inquiries with major customers and vendors as well as professional advisors. Files and records covering these major relationships may be the focus of study along with documents covering existing bank and equipment loans.

Usually when a large funding request is involved no stone will be left unturned. The credit standing of the principal owners of a business could be scrutinized especially if their personal guarantees are pledged to collateralize financing. Depending on the extent of collateral pledges there may be a physical examination of inventory, equipment, and machinery. Lastly, documents relating to valuable property rights such as licenses, leases and royalties may be reviewed.

Usually when a large funding request is involved no stone will be left unturned.

Just as entrepreneurs, CEOs and managers regularly devote significant time to operational matters of importance, they must continually assess their company's financial strengths and weaknesses in anticipation of an outsider's due diligence. The objective is not only to identify areas that could surface in these discussions but to reveal defects that could impact financial stability and profitability. It is always best to devise a plan to remedy underlying defects before they become a target for criticism.

At the early stage, it is important to understand that financiers initially distinguish high and low investment grade opportunities by reference to certain common rules of thumb, a few of which are listed below:

- A debt-to-worth ratio that exceeds 4-to-1 may be a sign of too heavy debt load.
- Accounts payable in excess of cash in banks, accounts receivable and inventory may indicate higher risk of insolvency.
- Inventory stock sixty days over pending customer orders may be a sign of declining marketability of merchandise inventory.
- Increased overall labor costs after a period of flat or declining sales may be indicative of poor financial management controls.
- Persistent bank overdrafts may be a sign of an undercapitalized business.
- Loan to value (LTV) of assets in excess of 70% to 80 % may indicate that equity capital is more suitable than debt funding.

After these types of basic assessments a more in depth evaluation is usually conducted. Understandably, investors and bankers want rule out any insurmountable health problems.

Norms and Benchmarks

A very reliable sign of the financial health of a business is how well it scores in relation to financial norms and standards within its own industry. These vital signs are considered highly indicative of a strong or weak performing company.

For the most part, a business is expected to demonstrate their worth when stacked against their peers. Passing the test can be tough to pass because some frontrunners may enjoy a capital and operating advantage that allows them to function more efficiently. Nevertheless, up and comers should be able to register high marks for operating versatility, cost efficiency and return on investment.

Peer data including industry and trade association information is almost universally relied on to grade a company's strategies and tactics. Even up and comers are expected to register high marks. Pertinent data is ordinarily segmented based on dollar ranges of assets and revenues. In order to be a strong candidate for bank and investor financing it is wise to work toward meeting financial norms and standards within the applicable asset size and revenue ranges. All things being equal, you do not want to allow your business to fall too far behind the pack.

When stacked next to the income statement of companies in your company's particular industry both positive and negative qualities are more detectable. For example, if your computer system and design services company's net income to sales percentage is significantly less than the six percent assuming that to be the norm, this may be indicative of operating weakness. At a minimum, both a financier and business owner would be interested in investigating the circumstances. In this sense, peer norms help to facilitate constructive discussion.

On the other hand, just because a company is out of step with industry norms does not necessarily mean it is underperforming. There may be valid and compelling business reasons for deviation. For example, a decision to rent more warehouse space in anticipation of a future contract could impose a higher than average rent expense. Similarly, it may be incumbent to pay higher wage rates based on competitive pay ranges within a certain geographic region. Generally speaking, these type of explanations rule out what might otherwise be a negative finding.

Some companies adopt business models dramatically different their more traditional competitors, resulting in significantly different than performance indicators. Regardless of how unique a firm is, however, a strong financial position is critical for success. In fact, financial strength can give a firm freedom to try new and innovative business concepts, as is the case with Patagonia.

> *Patagonia, maker of high quality outdoor clothing and gear, is considered one of the most innovative companies in the world. The firm is committed to environmental responsibility; Forbes magazine labeled it "the do-no-evil"[1] outdoor-apparel company and the "coolest company on the planet."[2] However, Patagonia founder and world-class mountaineer Yvon Chouinard knows accolades do not take the place of running a profitable venture.*
>
> *If we wish to lead corporate America by example, we have to be profitable. No company will respect us, no matter how much money we give away or how much publicity we receive for being one of the '100 Best Companies,' if we are not profitable. It's okay to be eccentric, as long as you are rich; otherwise you're just crazy.*[2]
>
> *The company distributes its eco-friendly products worldwide in more than 50 company-owned stores, at approximately 1,000 other retail outlets, and via catalog and online sales. Revenues consistently grew between 6% and 10% per year in the last decade, in both good and bad economic times, and total sales reached $333 million. At the high point, Patagonia's wholesale division generated revenues of $145 million and 45% gross margins. Company owned stores generated sales of $75 million and gross margins of over 68%.*[3]
>
> *The company is guided by its mission statement, "To build the best product, cause no unnecessary harm, and use business to inspire and implement solutions to the environmental crisis." Since inception Patagonia has donated 1% of its revenues to environmental causes, provided in-kind donations to environmental groups, and invested thousands of dollars into reducing the environmental impact of its production process.*
>
> *The firm introduced its Product Life Cycle Initiative, an attempt to take responsibility for the impact of its products on the environment from cradle to grave. In its "Don't Buy this Jacket" campaign, Patagonia encourages customers to limit their consumption of goods to only essential products and to choose well-made, long-lasting garments. Customers are encouraged to repair products as many times as possible to lengthen useful life, and Patagonia offers repair services for free or little cost. The company also facilitates reuse of Patagonia products by establishing an online swap market (partnering with eBay), donating*

useful products to environmental charities and recycling worn out apparel. Patagonia covers the cost of returning worn items for repair and recycling.

The initiative was very successful and helped grow Patagonia sales 30%, to $500 million within 12 months of its initiation.[2] The increased revenue, however, has not been the only reason for Patagonia's continued success. According to Chouinard, Patagonia is able to innovate and take risks because of its strong financial underpinnings.

- *The company carries very little debt; long term debt was just 2.2% of equity by year-end.[1]*
- *Its profit margins are stronger than most competitors. Gross margins average 55% of sales firmwide, allowing the company to absorb increased overhead associated with environmental efforts.[2]*
- *The company's cash position allows it to extend generous credit terms to wholesale accounts, thereby making it an attractive retail partner.*
- *Patagonia chooses its suppliers carefully and closely manages its supplier relationships; at one point the firm cut the number of outside suppliers from 200 to 41.[1]*
- *Patagonia has been able to charge a 20% premium for its products relative to its competitors, because Patagonia apparel is considered high quality, long lasting and environmentally responsible.[3]*

Chouinard summarizes his views on how to run a profitable business:

Strategic financial management has taught me another important lesson, never exceed your limits. You push the envelope and you live for those moments when you're right on the edge, but you don't go over. You have to be true to yourself; you have to know your strengths and limitations and live within your means.[4]

As the executives at Patagonia learned, routine reviews and comparisons of industry information offer a roadmap for improving financial returns. A bird's eye view of the business and financial performance of others could lead to the formulation of new strategies or reason to revise old ones. Tracking industry specific trends is not only a universal practice of financiers by an effective way for company management to evaluate its overall performance.

Generic Vital Signs

It is helpful to think of financial measures in terms of a MRI. Generally, they are designed to help detect and assess laden conditions. By analogy, in assessing a person's health, imaging feedback is sometimes used to spot abnormalities. By comparison in business, various financial markers are routinely confirmed to determine which, if any, of the important financial working parts are out of alignment.

There are at least a dozen financial measures of a generic nature that are considered crucial to check on a regular basis. Specifically, liquidity, cash flow, asset turnover, debt capacity, earnings and operating efficiency makers should receive special attention. Each metric is linked to at least one of the three basic financial statements, namely, the balance sheet, income statement and statement of cash flow.

It is wise for every key decision maker to have a basic understanding and knowledge of these generic vital signs. A proper application and interpretation is key for any business bent on attracting financing. Much like basic financial statements, these metrics belong in every entrepreneur's management handbook.

For ease of interpretation the more generic vital signs are described and illustrated below based on the sample financial statements in Chapter Five.

Ratio Names	Explanations and Uses	Ratio Formulas	Matrix *
Accounts Receivables:			
Accounts Receivable Ratio:	Turning over accounts receivable rapidly builds working capital and nurtures a positive cash flow. A turnover ratio measures the length of time required to record and collect payment on credit sales.	Net Credit Sales ÷ Average A/R	24 turns
Average Days Sales in Accounts Receivables	This ratio measures how many days worth of sales are tied up in accounts receivables and indicates how efficiently you are collecting from customers.	365 Days ÷ Accounts Receivable Turnover Ratio	15 days
Inventory Management:			
Turnover Ratio	The average length of time it takes to turn merchandise into customer sales affects working capital. Turnover ratio measures the number of times inventory is turned over during a specified period.	Cost of Goods Sold÷ Average Inventory	10 turns
Cash Flow Management:			
Long-Term Debt	This ratio measures the sufficiency of cash flow from operations to cover debt payment obligations.	Long-Term Debt Payments ÷ Cash From Operations	0.13
Debt Coverage	This ratio measures the sufficiency of cash flow from operations to cover total debt.	Total Debt ÷ Cash From Operations	0.72
Cash Flow to Sales	This ratio measures the efficiency with which sales result in cash flow.	Cash From Operations ÷ Sales	0.09
Operational Index	This ratio measures the relationship between cash flow generated during a period and net income during the same period.	Cash From Operations ÷ Net Income	1.78
Cash Flow to Debt	Many analysts feel that this ratio is the best single indicator of a firm's solvency. A rough view of cash flow is net income plus depreciation.	(New Income + Depreciation) ÷ Total Debt	1.39

Ratio Names	Explanations and Uses	Ratio Formulas	Matrix *
Interest Coverage:			
Times Interest Earned	The Times Interest Earned ratio is a valuable tool in analyzing leverage financing. It provides for the relationship between earnings and interest charges. This ratio measures the number of times that interest cost is earned by a company as a result of its operations. The higher the ratio the stronger the coverage. A minimum ratio is 1 to 1; a typical guideline is from 3 to 1.	Earnings Before Interest and Taxes ÷ Total Interest	20.59
Total Interest coverage	This ratio analyzes the firm's ability to repay interest and make the principal periodic repayments. This ratio clearly indicates to the banker the firm's cash flow available for debt service.	(Earnings Before Interest and Taxes) ÷ (Total Interest + Principal Payments)	5.93
Rates of Return:			
Return on Equity	Measures how effectively owner and investor funds are leveraged to generate income.	Net Income (during a period of time) ÷ Net Worth (at beginning of period)	
Return on Assets	Measures how effectively a company leverages all its assets (both current and long-term) to generate income.	Net Income (during a period of time) ÷ Total Assets (at beginning of period)	

*** Reference financial statements in Chapter 5**

Financial ratios are analogous to player stats. In baseball, hitters evaluate their batting average, pitchers the number of earned runs allowed, and base runners their steals versus the number of attempts.

In professional football quarterbacks study their passing attempts and completions; running backs their carries and average yards; and receivers their receptions and yards gained after the catch. Just as these statistics help athletes to evaluate and improve their performance, a regular review of your company's financial vital signs holds this potential benefit as well.

Financial Safeguards

Safeguards over the finances of a business are commonly referred to as internal controls. They are designed to help minimize risk for undetected accounting errors, fraud and other financial irregularities. Because many small but growing businesses lean heavy on a few people to administer the accounting functions of the business, adequate safeguards are crucial. Indeed, even many large companies fall victim to crippling errors and fraud when their system of checks and balances falls apart.

At the outset of this chapter I raised a hypothetical scenario involving a business owner who discovered certain unexplained electronic fund transfers in their company bank account. There is always a possibility under these circumstances that an odd looking item may be just the tip of the iceberg. Therefore, immediate action must be taken to identify any improprieties but just as important, develop financial controls and safeguards to prevent future damage.

In the midst of developing a business and dealing with a litany of demands, business owners may be less inclined to pay attention to the need for strong financial safeguards. In fact, most fraud occurs because the owner is preoccupied and as a result, places most financial related duties and responsibilities in the hands of a single individual. To counter the risk a system of cross-checking, physical verification and close monitoring is highly recommended. At the core, financial accounting duties and responsibilities should be divided among several different people in a manner that requires cross checking in their normal routine.

Separation of duties is the most essential internal control concept. The goal is to deter theft and fraud as well as detect errors. These types of procedures work to minimize the possibility that someone in the management or administrative processing chain will make an intentional or unintentional error without notice. Needless to say no company can thrive monetarily where financial errors, improprieties or misdeeds are permitted without repercussion. History is replete with both small and large businesses that collapsed or suffered from financial frauds and indiscretions.

Legislation makes internal control review and improvement a requirement for publicly owned companies. The Sarbanes-Oxley Act enacted into law in 2002 regulates issues such as corporate governance and financial reporting, and it penalizes public companies for inaccurate or incomplete financial disclosure. Sarbanes-Oxley also stipulates public companies must subject themselves to a comprehensive review of their internal controls no more than 90 days before releasing material financial information relating to the company and its consolidated subsidiaries. This legislation epitomizes the cliché, "trust but verify."

Nowadays, internal control examinations are considered best practices for public companies. Adopting this practice as a means of quality assurance also could prove beneficial for entrepreneurial companies as well. Internal controls designed to promote better financial security paramount for asset protection. The fundamental objectives of these type or policies and procedures include:

- Safeguard assets from misuse or misappropriation.
- Verify that business resources were utilized for business purposes only.
- Maintain reliable record keeping systems that promote financial reporting accuracy.
- Promote compliance with control policies and procedures.

As earlier suggested small businesses often struggle to accomplish these objectives with only a few staff persons. In some cases, the owner may have to continually be the source of direct authorization, approval and review of certain financial translations. In any environment, the following general guidelines could be helpful in strengthening a basic system of internal controls:

CUSTOMER REMITTANCES

- Consider bonding employees who handle substantial amounts of cash.
- Route incoming customer remittances to someone other than the person responsible for maintaining the accounting system and posting bank deposits.
- Customer remittances received should be stamped "for deposit only."
- Bank deposits should be made on a daily basis and funds secured until deposited.
- Over-the-counter cash collections should be tracked and accounted for at the end of each shift.

DISBURSEMENT OF FUNDS

- Persons with bank signature should not have access to restricted accounting duties and responsibilities.
- Bank statements should be reviewed and reconciled monthly by someone not responsible for making deposits or processing checks.
- Accounting related documents such as customer invoices and bank checks should be pre-numbered to assure accountability.
- Bank signatory authority should be highly restricted.
- Access to accounting software and other systems should be highly restricted.
- Payments should be approved only with an invoice or other documentation.

PETTY CASH OVERSIGHT

- Custody of petty cash should be limited.
- Supporting voucher requests should be used to authorize disbursements.

- The fund should be counted and reconciled on a regular basis by someone other than the custodian.
- A dollar balance ceiling should be established.
- A reconciliation of supporting vouchers, invoices and other documentation should be performed regularly by someone other than the custodian.

RECEIVABLES ADMINISTRATION

- Customer purchase orders, billing statements and shipping documents should be maintained.
- A reconciliation of activity based on the documents noted should be performed.

PAYROLL PROCESSING

- Employee hires and terminations should be verified independently.
- Access to payroll processing systems and records should be highly restricted.
- Payroll should not be processed by those responsible for processing hires and terminations.

ACCOUNTING FOR INVENTORY EQUIPMENT

- Physical inventories should be taken on a regular basis.
- High dollar items should be tracked and accounted for by serial number.
- Physical counts and values should be reconciled to accounting records.

Second Opinions

In most cases an assurance regarding your company's financial statements from an outside third party can be extremely beneficial. An outside perspective serves as another type of internal control regarding the accounting and financial reporting process. Additionally, whether you employ one person or a department to handle accounting functions an outsider will provide, at a minimum, another level of review.

There is growing pressure on companies of all sizes to become more accountable for generating high quality and reliable financial statements. More businesses are engaging CPAs to provide a written assurance about the fair presentation of their financial statements. The professional opinion of a CPA adds credibility to the numbers and thereby comfort to outside stakeholders.

The CPA's written opinion principally speaks to a company's adherence to GAAP. In this regard, CPAs provide three types of assurance services. From lowest to highest these assurances are labeled compilation, review and audit. In each case, the CPA provides a written report that accompanies the financial statements and reporting. A snapshot of these underlying processes is provided on the following page.

A compilation is the representation of management (the owners) and is limited to presenting in the form of financial statements. CPAs do not audit or review the financial statements and, accordingly, do not express an opinion or any other form of assurance on them.

A review consists principally of inquiries of company personnel and analytical procedures applied to financial data. It is substantially less in scope than an audit in accordance with generally accepted auditing standards, the objective of which is the expression of an opinion regarding the financial statements taken as a whole. Accordingly, CPAs do not express such as opinion.

An audit includes examining, on a test basis, evidence supporting the amounts and disclosures in the financial statements. An audit also includes assessing the accounting principles used for significant estimates made by management, as well as evaluating the overall financial statement presentation. Audits provide a reasonable basis for CPAs opinion on whether the financial statements are presented fairly in all material respects.

INDEPENDENT AUDITOR'S REPORT

To the Board of Directors
Matrix, Inc.
Baltimore, Maryland

Report on the Financial Statements

We have audited the accompanying financial statements of ABC Company which comprise of the balance sheets as of December 31, 20X1 and 20X0, and the related statements of income, changes in stockholders' equity, and cash flows for the years then ended, and the related notes to the financial statements.

Management's Responsibility for the Financial Statements

Management is responsible for the preparation and fair presentation of these financial statements in accordance with accounting principles generally accepted in the United States of America; this includes the design, implementation, and maintenance of internal control relevant to the preparation and fair presentation of financial statements that are free from material misstatement, whether due to fraud or error.

Auditor's Responsibility

Our responsibility is to express an opinion on these financial statements based on our audits. We conducted our audits in accordance with auditing standards generally accepted in the United States of America. Those standards require that we plan and perform the audit to obtain reasonable assurance about whether the financial statements are free from material misstatement.

An audit involves performing procedures to obtain audit evidence about the amounts and disclosures in the financial statements. The procedures selected depend on the auditor's judgment, including the assessment of the risks of material misstatement of the financial statements, whether due to fraud or error. In making those risk assessments, the auditor considers internal control relevant to the entity's preparation and fair presentation of the financial statements in order to design audit procedures that are appropriate in the circumstances, but not for the purpose of expressing an opinion on the effectiveness of the entity's internal control. Accordingly, we express no such opinion. An audit also includes evaluating the appropriateness of accounting policies used and the reasonableness of significant accounting estimates made by management, as well as evaluating the overall presentation of the financial statements. We believe that the audit evidence we have obtained is sufficient and appropriate to provide a basis for our audit opinion.

Opinion

In our opinion, the financial statements referred to above present fairly, in all material respects, the financial position of ABC Company as of December 31, 20Xl and 20X0, and the results of their operations and their cash flows for the years then ended in accordance with accounting principles generally accepted in the United States of America.

The Hutt Co., LLC
Columbia, Maryland
March 1, 20X1 and 20X0

To best appreciate the end result of an audit, a sample of a standard unqualified opinion is presented on the previous page.

For any company anticipating a public or private stock offering in the near future a financial statement audit is highly recommended. Audited financial statements are usually required by regulators who oversee private and public offerings. On the other hand, a "review" or "compilation" may be acceptable for privately-owned businesses which take on no more than bank financing.

From a cost perspective, compilations and reviews are generally less expensive than audits because the CPA's scope of work is not nearly as extensive. Neither one entails an in-depth inspection, testing, nor analytical work called for in an audit. At a bare minimum, compilations are generally advised for small businesses with no major outside financing.

NOTABLE REFLECTIONS AT A GLANCE

- Financial health measurements comprise conventional financial percentages and ratios.
- Critical vital signs include financial liquidity, profitability, cash flow, asset turnover and debt capacity.
- Performance comparisons allow businesses to be ranked and evaluated.
- Rules of thumb determine financial wellness based on debt to equity, accounts receivable turnover and other financial relationships.
- Assurances from CPAs in the form of compilation, review and audit add credibility to financial statements.
- Financial checks and balances safeguard assets and deter misuse.

CHAPTER EIGHT

Finance the Dream... Accelerate the Breakthrough

| *The Journey* |

In the past, Mediclean relied solely on debt financing to raise capital. BJ did not want to entertain the prospect of partner investment because of his strong reservations about sharing ownership and control. However, he now realizes his company may have grown faster and more profitability had he been more flexible in his thinking.

Taylor Made—having experienced a leveling off in sales growth—believes equity funding could provide the resources necessary for her to pursue emerging business opportunities with less worry about short-term cash flow. She is committed to fully evaluating the pros and cons of equity capital versus debt financing. She is also interested in identifying not only individuals but venture funds and other types of financiers.

"Financing your business with other people's money" is a widely used but quite misleading cliché. Financing a business is not a simple matter. Investors and banks will not flock to the aid of a business venture just for the sake of it. Just like any other business association based on sound economics, the marriage must be a win-win proposition for both sides.

In order to secure financing which in large part may be with other people's money, a CEO has to prepare to leap through a series of hoops. The gauntlet of questions and document requests serve to provide financiers with a deeper understanding of the financial profile of a business, the reasons financing is necessary and the prospects for return on investment. Rarely, will this process be a slam dunk. Even after receiving financing approval, there will be a battery of stiff conditions, qualifications and strings attached. These hurdles will show no shortage for a need for close scrutiny.

Just like entrepreneurs, a financer's intent is to grow their bottom line through maximizing return on their investment. This principle applies to private investors, bankers and other types of financiers. To forge a lucrative alliance you should never lose sight of the underlying incentive to "do a deal."

For a CEO the hunt for capital requires intense preparation, strategic planning and attention to detail. At a minimum the leader of the enterprise will be expected to outline of a credible business plan which in most cases should be in written form. When seeking debt, projected cash from operations shown in the business plan should reflect a level of sufficiency necessary to cover scheduled monthly debt payments. On the other hand, when investment capital is involved, future cash flows must show the potential for investor payouts or dividends.

After identifying financing needs companies seeking financing should prepare to demonstrate a capacity to meet ongoing financial reporting requirements. At a minimum lenders and investors will insist that the company in which they invest periodically provide a reliable set of financial statements.

The investee or borrower must be on guard and alert especially at the front end of the deal. A litany of limitations or restrictions will most likely be proposed within the contractual framework. These provisions should be carefully reviewed and thoughtfully evaluated prior to closing by the management team as well as a CPA and business attorney.

In their excitement and zeal to obtain funding, CEOs and entrepreneurs especially sometimes minimize the legal and operational burdens brought to bear by a financing relationship. Indeed, there may be an inclination simply to gloss over contractual details. The danger of course, legal details could later prove to be unduly one-sided, too expensive to administer or overly restrictive. Truth is, from the investee or borrower perspective the fine print in financing agreements often sours the perceived benefit of the deal.

The terms and conditions for financing is where the negotiation is won or lost. Thoughtful bargaining must be used to avoid provisions that could become onerous over time including an unreasonably low ceiling of maximum funding, ill timing of any balloon payments, too many restrictions over the use of collateral, and penalties if any for early pay-off. Make no mistake—when it comes to financing—there are no free lunches. Before seriously bidding for financing a CEO is wise to gain a clear understanding of financing alternatives, underwriting protocols, and financial reporting requirements.

CHAPTER HIGHLIGHTS:

- Common Types of Business Financing
- Understanding and Quantifying Financing Needs
- Criteria for Selecting a Financing Partner
- Shopping Your Deal
- Preparing a Successful Financing Request

The Fast Track

For most companies access to financing is an imperative. Without access to capital, even the most promising business could languish between making just enough to pay the bills and not enough to take the company one step higher. One of the best examples of how to rapidly build strong financing relationships in a short span of time is Google.

Google was founded in 1996 by two Stanford University graduate students, Larry Page and Sergey Brin. Unable to afford new computers, the pair worked on borrowed University equipment, funded expenses on credit cards, and located their first data center in Larry's dorm room. Initially the pair sought to license their technology to an outside party.

When existing companies rejected the partners' licensing offer, Larry and Sergey decided to further develop the technology in their own firm. They needed cash to set up a commercial space and repay their credit cards. A friend of a faculty member believed the company had a great deal of potential and invested $100,000 in Google. Ultimately the company raised $1 million in its first round of equity financing.

By early 1999 Google had moved twice, first to a garage and then to an office building. It was answering more than 500,000 queries a day and had been named one of the world's Top 100 Web Sites by PC magazine. Additional funding was needed to keep Google expanding.

In June 1999 Google secured $25 million in funding from two venture capital firms. Each firm took a seat on the Google board of directors and the board became populated with individuals who had helped grow Sun Mircrosystems, Intuit, Amazon and Yahoo!. Key employees were hired and the firm continued to expand.

Google continued to mature by improving its technology, entering into partnerships with other internet service providers and adding products such as Google News, AdWords and Google Compute. Its growth has been explosive.

In 2004, Google's owners decided to take the company public. The initial public offering ("IPO") raised roughly $1.7 billion, making it the largest internet IPO of its time and one of the largest IPOs in history. The IPO provided cash for expansion and enabled early investors to cash out. [1]

In the span of just six years, Goggle progressed from a mom and pop operation to a publicly traded corporation valued at roughly $23 billion. Most importantly, the company's ascent would not have materialized without sufficient capital financing.

Perhaps the most notable thing about the Goggle story is the evolving financing strategies. As highlighted in the synopsis, the company utilized different financing methods and toggled between various financing sources. Your particular strategy may differ, however, Google provides basic, helpful lessons to take away. A search for alternative financing could be prompted by the opportunity to lower interest rates or to secure a higher credit limit. On the other hand, the best funding for start up businesses could come from friends and family. A business that strategically refinances its debt could free up its cash flow. Regardless of your motivation, the financing approaches discussed in this chapter should be helpful.

The Turning Point

The very discussion of financing sometimes triggers a plethora of reaction among business leaders, both positive and negative. Despite their differences of opinions, most business people agree that the more you know about the rules of the game in advance, the more likely you will be successful.

A common discovery is how challenging it is for a newly-formed business to attract capital. Most banks frown on start-ups because they lack a past financial track record of earnings. Most agree at least with respect to start-ups, banks are more risk adverse compared to the private and public investor community.

In virtually every instance, financiers will want a clear explanation of how they will be repaid for loaning their money. This is every financier's underlying concern regardless of the company's stage of development, business or industry. For example, most start up companies tap into personal savings to finance their business' launch. Some are even fortunate to have family and friends chip in with financial support. However, as a business picks up steam in terms of sales growth it will inevitably need some form of outside financing. A financier will want to gauge the strength of the company's sales demand and prospects for sustaining growth.

A financier will also study the reasons a business seeks financing. A build up in accounts receivable could be the impetus for a company to seek bank financing. However, the financier will also ascertain whether there are latent operating deficiencies in the business. Such could be the case in a business that extends customer credit without requiring routine credit checks. To confirm the company's financial health status, the financier may also analyze the company's financial statements, financial ratios, as well as any projections.

Typically, businesses seek financiers to help fund new equipment and expansion. However businesses may also seek financing because of slow customer remittances. In many situations, customer remittances arrive too late to provide the cash needed to pay creditors by the payment due date. Unless a company receives some type of financing for cash flow, this timing differential will burn through its cash reserves.

Business growth and development also spurs the need for various forms of financing. Normally, sales growth normally pressures a business' cash reserves in a variety of ways. Increasing demand for products or services also escalate a business' production and facilities costs. These costs could also include costs to meet infrastructure requirements. Eventually, many businesses find it necessary to acquire more space and facilities. As it pertains to the financing process, fast growing entrepreneurial companies like Google have to mature in a relatively short span of time.

Fast growing businesses quickly have to weigh their financing options; equity, debt, or most commonly some combination thereof. The term "debt" refers to funds provided to a business at a specific interest rate with a definite and immediate repayment. The interest rate may be fixed or variable, and repayment may be in installments or in full. Financers typically require collateral to support debt repayment.

"Equity" generally refers to money contributed by outsiders to a business under a flexible repayment schedule or that has no repayment timetable. The expectation is that repayment of investment will come from profits, sale of the company's assets, merger with another company or a significant refinancing. Because of its inherent risks, equity investors typically request the right to vote and participate in a company's business affairs.

Whether you operate a new or mature business, there are financing has many dos and don'ts just pertaining to the amount of funding you request. Many wonder whether they should request what they need in funds, whether they should search for capital before (or after) financing needs arise, and whether they should seek debt or equity capital. We will address these key issues that will be addressed in the remainder of this chapter.

Equity refers to money contributed by outsiders to a business under a flexible repayment schedule or that has no repayment timetable.

Raising Equity

Generally, equity offers a more flexible repayment structure than debt. Depending on the circumstances and needs the equity option may be more desirable for a variety of reasons. Investors accept greater risks with equity. With equity, financer's return on their money is closely tied to the earnings of the business. Typically, there is no specific term or date for repayment. Additionally, Equity investors tend to be less fixated on historical financial results and more focused on a business' forecasted financial performance.

Pursuing equity capital is an important element of raising large sums of investment dollars. Capital intensive businesses known to frequently tap capital markets include, but are not limited to, real estate, manufacturing, technology and research and development markets. Equity investors are more apt to take chances. In exchange for their willingness, they usually insist on more direct participation and/or oversight in business matters.

Many businesses that became icons overnight were launched with equity capital. Owners raised millions of dollars selling stock in the public market and utilized the funds to generate enormous financial gains. "Going public" refers to selling equity interests in a company to the general public, typically with the assistance of an investment banker. There are stringent requirements for going public. Only a small percentage of companies meet these requirements. As such, only a relative few choose this route.

Along the journey a company must pay dividends to its investors. They represent a distribution of earnings to owners (shareholders) of a corporation. In most states, payment of dividends is discretionary by law. A majority of the board of directors must vote in favor of a payout after considering its current profits, accumulated earnings and future business needs. Similarly, in a limited liability company, leftover earnings are technically available for distribution to owners (members).

Venture funds are a special subset of equity financing most germane to entrepreneurial businesses. Unlike public equity financers, venture capitalists seek investment opportunities with early stage and start-up companies. Often, the risk of failure is higher, but the potential for significant financial returns is strongest. Venture funding sources are well-suited for a company with a marginal financial history but solid prospects for future growth and earnings. Moreover, venture capitalists place great emphasis on growth potential and less, to some extent, on past performance.

Venture capital typically is made available through the auspices of a venture fund created on behalf of pension funds, institutional investors, and high net worth individuals. Generally, venture funds invest $1 million or more in companies growing at a rate of 50% or more each year. A sub-class of these investors are known as "angel investors." Angel investors provide private equity on a smaller scale. Often, angel investors often will consider smaller deals (those under $1 million) as well as larger ones as funds allow.

There are high performance expectations associated with venture capital funding. Most venture capital funds aim to double, triple or possibly quadruple in value within five to seven years. To further their prospects for success, these investors typically seek active participation in management and may insist on a seat on the company's board of directors.

Given the high level of financial risk assumed by venture capital investors, it is no surprise these deals often entail a legal options that protect investors. These options may include options that allow the investor to exit via a buyout or acquire additional shares of ownership after a specified period. These options are referred to as "puts" and "calls." Through a "put," the investor reserves the legal right to force the owner to purchase its shares at a predetermined price. By using a "put," if the company fails to significantly increase the value, sells its assets, or goes public, an investor may recover. On the other hand, investors may consent to a "call provision" permits the company to force the investor to return its shares at a predetermined price if the company exceeds its growth and earnings targets.

Because venture capital funds are highly selective in making investments and only a very small percentage of entrepreneurs who submit proposals receive a favorable response, the majority of entrepreneurial companies pursue investments from either family and friends or conventional debt financing.

The Debt Leverage

In comparison to equity, debt financing involves more repayment terms and assets pledged as collateral. Commercial loans typically include obligations to repay the principal loan amount, plus interest on a monthly basis until the balance is fully paid. The interest rate and repayment schedule may vary widely from one type of lender to the next.

In the event of default, lenders generally reserve the right to take possession of assets pledged as collateral. Most entrepreneurs and small business owners in tight-knit companies typically pledge personal assets as collateral. In addition to giving a personal guarantee, this means personal financial exposure is most at risk.

However, the value and extent of personal collateral is not the sole determination in business lending. Even with worthy collateral, most lenders will not approve a loan unless there is a relatively low risk of default. Commercial lenders prefer borrowers with an ability to generate more than enough earnings to service the loan.

Purveyors of debt capital safeguard their investments by also requiring the borrower to demonstrate an ability to repay a loan from earnings. At the same time, a pledge of collateral functions as insurance for a loan. Sources of collateral may include real estate, equipment, inventory, accounts receivable and marketable securities. When there is a deficiency in repayment, lenders commonly invoke collateral rights or a personal guarantee in order to recover.

In some communities, publicly sponsored economic development agencies provide loan guarantees to eligible businesses. The agent is a "guarantor" for the business and makes a private or public guarantee. That guarantee obligates the issuing party (the guarantor) to repay the loan in the event that the primary borrower (the business) defaults. This additional source of repayment may make lenders more comfortable and enable them to fund projects that they otherwise would turn down.

Prior to approving a loan, banks scrutinize company cash flows, earning projections and financial statements with great intensity.

Before approving a loan, banks scrutinize company cash flows, earning projections and financial statements with great intensity. Like equity investors, even after making a loan, commercial lenders actively monitor the borrower's financial performance. At a minimum, they require borrowers to submit financial statements and other performance reports annually, quarterly, and sometimes even weekly or monthly. These reporting requirements allow lenders to track borrowers' financial performance and resources.

The loan evaluation and negotiation process may be quite extensive and exhaustive. Unlike venture capital funds commercial lenders exert influence and control at the outset because they usually have little interaction with borrowers after funding the loan.

Menu a La Carte

Whenever there is a need for financing, the proverbial question is, "what type of financing makes the most sense?" When reviewing choices and alternatives, note the following simple ground rules:

Short-term financing should only be used where money is needed for a period of one year or less; intermediate term, for one to five years; and long-term, for more than five years. Based on these guidelines an appropriate repayment period parallels the life span of the underlying asset being financed or, in case of working capital, a time period that corresponds with projected future earnings.

To illustrate, if a business intends to borrow funds to purchase vehicles, the minimum financing term should be at least three and possibly five years. Since the equipment involved has a beneficial life cycle of several years or more, the appropriate term of financing should be in the intermediate range. On the other hand, if the purpose of the funding is to liquefy accounts receivable, the funding mechanism should be short term and tailored to accommodate normal turnover of between 30 to 60 days. If a significant portion of the customer base consists of government agencies, then normal turnover can be up to 90 days.

To avoid financing misalignment, entrepreneurs should review reevaluate their debt portfolio on a regular basis. I summarize common debt financing alternatives below.

WORKING CAPITAL LINE OF CREDIT	A line of credit is one of the most common financing vehicles available to small companies. The LOC consists of a specific sum made available by a bank to a qualifying company to draw on as needed over a prescribed period, usually one year. Typically the borrower is required to repay the line periodically, then the firm may reuse the funds.
ACCOUNTS RECEIVABLE FINANCING	Accounts receivable financing is a loan that uses accounts receivable as the primary source of repayment. The lender usually advances 70% to 80% of the adjusted accounts receivable balance. The business can repay and re-borrow any amount up to the agreed upon percentage of its adjusted accounts receivable balance.
FACTORING	Factoring is a purchase of accounts receivable as they arise. The business submits orders as they are received to the factor for approval. In turn the factor advances the funds (less a discount for bad accounts and a financing charge) to the business. Receivables are paid directly to the factorer.

TERM FINANCING

Term loans are available in a variety of forms and are structured according to the length of use of the item(s) for which the proceeds will be applied. They also reflect repayment conditions consistent with availability of the primary sources of repayment. Most often obtained for equipment purchases such as computers, vehicles, furniture and machinery.

ASSET-BASED BORROWING

Most simplistically asset based lending refers to any loan secured by an asset. Mortgages and receivables factoring are asset based loans. Usually, however, asset based lending is used to describe loans secured by assets not normally used to secure loans. Intellectual property and trademarks may be collateral for asset based loans. Typically, these loans are riskier and more expensive than other types of financing.

MORTGAGE BORROWING

Mortgage loans are generally long-term loans with maturities of 15 years or more secured by real property.

"Bread and Butter" Issues

A strong case for financing answers three key questions: 1) "Why does your company need financing?" 2) "How much funding does your company require?" and 3) "How and when will you repay the funds?" A company that is prepared to unequivocally answer these questions has a stronger chance of obtaining funding.

BASIC FINANCING NEEDS

When company first discovers a need for additional funding, the underlying factors may not be obvious. Gaining a clear understanding and breakdown may require careful and thoughtful analysis. I list some common possibilities below:

START-UP/ MOBILIZATION CAPITAL

Funds required to purchase goods and services to launch a business. Purchases typically are one-time in nature and include legal and accounting fees to establish an enterprise, office equipment, and marketing material development.

WORKING CAPITAL	Cash needed to fund day to day operations including salaries, rent and marketing costs over a period of time, such as a year.
ACCOUNTS RECEIVABLE	Funds needed as an advance against existing eligible accounts receivable (normally those no more than 90 days due).
INVENTORY	Funds needed to acquire inventory (including pieces for assembly for future sale).
EQUIPMENT	Funds needed for equipment for all aspects of the business, including manufacturing equipment, computers, and copiers.
REAL ESTATE	Funding for acquisition of real estate to be held for business use.
BUSINESS ACQUISITION	Funds used to acquire assets of an existing business. May include funding for inventory, equipment, customer lists and goodwill.

AMOUNT OF FINANCING REQUIRED

Once a company identifies the purpose of financing, the next step is to quantify the amount of money needed. The goal is for the prospective financier to reach the same conclusion regarding the necessary amount of financing. Remember, the business applicant has to make a compelling pitch to the prospective financer.

At minimum, a company should include a comprehensive cash flow projection to support the amount of financing it seeks. Depending on the nature of funding, however, additional transaction-specific cash analyses may be necessary. For example, a summary of average accounts receivable and accounts payable turnover may be appropriate in the case of receivables financing. The illustration on the following page shows a sample cash analysis involving accounts receivables and payables.

In the hypothetical case presented, it is logical to conclude the company needs financing in the range of $80,000 ($40,000 month 1 and $40,000 month 2) to pay expenses as they become due.

Accounts Receivable Financing Analysis

	Month 1	Month 2	Month 3
Sales – Billings	$100,000	$300,000	$500,000
Collections			
Current	20,000	60,000	100,000
> 30 Days	0	50,000	150,000
> 60 Days	0	0	30,000
> 90 Days	0	0	0
Total Est. Collections	20,000	110,000	280,000
Accounts Payable	$60,000	$180,000	$300,000
Payments			
Current	30,000	90,000	150,000
> 30 Days		30,000	90,000
> 60 Days			
> 90 Days			
Notes Payable	10,000	10,000	10,000
Other	20,000	20,000	30,000
Total Est. Disbursements	$60,000	$150,000	$260,000
Summary			
Collections	$20,000	$110,000	$280,000
Disbursements	60,000	150,000	260,000
Net Cash from Operations	($40,000)	($40,000)	$20,000

SOURCE AND TIMING OF REPAYMENT

A financing proposal should also specify the anticipated time and method of loan repayment or distribution of earnings to investors. I provide general guidelines to consider below:

Often companies repay loans from operating profits. For example, cash from operations covers contract financing, inventory purchases and financing for receivables. Monthly cash flow, however, is not the only source of repayment. Be sure to inform your banker or investor if repayment depends on future refinancing or asset sales.

Financing Purpose	Normal Period of Repayment
Start-up/Mobilization Capital	6-24 months
Working Capital	1-5 years
Accounts Receivable	1 year revolving
Inventory	1 year revolving
Equipment	3-7 years
Real Estate	15-25 years
Business Acquisition	5-10 years

Choosing a Financier

Business decision makers should be selective when choosing a financing partner. As most seasoned veterans recognize, this financing relationship is essentially a marriage. Just as you carefully choose and build close relationships, there are parallels with respects to choosing a financing partner.

An entrepreneur, during his or her start-up stage, may desire a personal and consultative relationship with his or her financing partner. This can be especially true when the businessperson has no prior experience. On the other hand, a more mature enterprise with a successful track record may have little or no need to interface with a financier. I've listed many of the practical considerations for selecting a financing partner are listed below:

- Do you need a financier who will provide technical assistance in addition to funding?
- Do you need a financier who offers ancillary services, such as payroll processing, cash management, lock box, direct deposit or electronic and internet banking services?
- Do you want a personal relationship with one individual who knows, understands and is in regular contact with your business?
- Do you prefer a basic money exchange relationship whereby funds are available for withdrawal when needed and repaid as required?
- Do you want a financier that has the capacity to finance your business needs as they evolve in the intermediate and long-term future?

Ideally, most companies start with a short list of financial prospects who match their needs and requirements. These financial prospects can range from family, friends, investors to commercial banks. The primary objective is to measure and match overall compatibility.

Lenders and venture capitalists usually specialize in specific industries and industry segments. They also differ with regard to what they consider acceptable use of funds. Some financiers may only disperse funds against accounts receivable, while other financers depend on tangible personal equipment and commercial real estate. Fortunately, the investment capital community is highly diverse. There is a match for virtually every type of need.

Familiarity with the types and practices of different types of financiers can help expedite the search for an acceptable financing partner. Specifically, knowledge of their particular fields of concentration, underwriting standards and pricing structures can easily separate prospective financers from suspect financers. Below, I provide the most likely candidates:

Common Sources of Financing and Investment

CROWD FUNDING

Crowd funding is a way to raise small amounts of capital for a project or venture from a large number of people via the internet. It is arguably the most efficient and effective way for an existing or newly minted entrepreneur to attract investment capital. Otherwise entrepreneurs may spend months canvassing through personal networks, vetting potential investors, and exerting time and money just to obtain an audience. Crowdfunding also offers the opportunity to secure more flexible funding terms and conditions. Investors may contribute thousands or as little as $20 in exchange for a first-run product or other reward.

COMMERCIAL BANKS

Commercial banks typically provide short and medium term debt financing. The majority of their loan portfolios constitute business lending. The cost of financing depends on the prevailing prime interest rate. Typically, loans are priced at two or more points above prime, depending on the business' overall credit evaluation.

LEASING COMPANIES

Leasing companies provide alternatives to debt and equity financing, especially for equipment. Sometimes leasing is a viable option to purchasing for reasons relating to income taxes, financing restrictions and obsolescence. Leases usually carry a built in or imputed interest factor slightly higher than commercial bank rates.

FACTORS

Factors are specialized commercial financing companies that make business loans indirectly by purchasing accounts receivable from borrowers. Factors charge a discount rate that equates to interest. The cost is depends on prevailing interest rates, the percent of uncollected receivables, and the company's historic performance. Typically, factoring is an expensive method of financing.

VENTURE CAPITAL FUNDS

Venture capital firms provide equity financing in exchange for a piece of ownership in the company. As a result, venture firms typically are willing to wait longer for their returns than are banking institutions. Funding generally ranges upward from $250,000, and requires 25% to 50% return on their investments each year. Returns can reach 500% over the life of the investment. The terms for financing vary widely among venture capital funds.

INVESTMENT BANKS

Investment banks help raise capital through public offerings of equity shares and corporate bonds of businesses. Generally, the investment banker assumes responsibility for selling the securities at a set price to the general public. Stock and bond prices depend on both market factors and overall economic conditions. Often stocks provide a dividend payable periodically at the discretion of the board of directors. Bonds offer a stated rate of interest, payable at periodic intervals, set accordingly to the bonds' rating, based on the company's credit history and future projections.

PUBLIC AND GOVERNMENT FINANCING PROGRAMS

Various federal, state and local government funds assist business owners with financing. Most funds share the objectives of job retention and new job creation. Some define eligibility by industry. Others define it by size. Many target businesses that cannot obtain traditional bank financing. Financial support varies by program and includes grants, direct loans, loan guarantees, contract financing and surety bonding. Ordinarily, public and governmental funding involves interest on direct loans, fees on loan guarantees and premiums on surety bonds. The rates vary widely depending on the source, use and term of the financing.

Most financiers distinguish themselves by their different appetites and preferences for certain types of financing. For example, it would be an unproductive for a company to seek venture capital to finance equipment costing less than $200,000. Similarly, it would not be wise to request a working capital loan with a leasing company. On the other hand, an investment bank may be the perfect match for a mature company with a history of stable earnings and desire to go public. Understanding different financiers' appetites saves you valuable time. It can also help you avoid unnecessary frustration.

Making the Cut

It can be exhausting and time consuming to complete the financing process successfully. Even a business with a positive record of earnings generally can expect to encounter stiff obstacles, resistance and perhaps rejection. While financial performance and future prospects weigh heavily, business leaders should keep in mind that a rejection could be precipitated by lack of financial documentation or no clear justification for the amount of funding requested.

Companies are also declined for financing in cases where financial statements contain material errors or the financial statements themselves do not appear to be prepared professionally. Financiers' often complain that financial statements not prepared professionally hamper their ability to thoroughly and responsibly evaluate business revenues, expenses, assets and liabilities. Whenever a financer's review falls short of a complete financial analysis, a company's chances of a favorable funding outcome are slim.

Often, serious discrepancies are sometimes tied to financial forecasts. A business' plan normally includes a financial projection. The company presents this plan to financers. Problems arise when the cash flow projection conflicts with historical data, market data and industry statistics. Financiers will be very skeptical whenever there is a blatant disparity with these critical factors. It is important to remember that these projections and plans speak volumes about your company. For the most part, you only get one opportunity to make a good first impression.

For a CEO's cash flow projection to be considered credible, it must reveal, explain, and support each underlying, key assumption. A financial forecast that lacks back up for pivotal figures is a "no-no." Every assumption should include an explanation and reasonably reflect market indicators, surveys, contracts or other metrics. Your revenue estimates should be consistent with historical financial performance and prevailing market conditions. You should explain major departures thoroughly. A financial forecast with atypical estimated spikes in revenue can raise serious concerns about creditability. For example, a revenue forecast that puts next year's revenue at $1,000,000 while the average for the prior three years was less than $500,000 will definetely cause concern.

Finally, bankers and investors will be inclined to pass on deals where projected operating expenses appear unreasonably low. For instance, a projection in which sales are estimated to increase more than 30% but operating and overhead expenses remain flat should also cause a potential lender to doubt reasonableness.

Designing a Dossier

Figuratively speaking, a financing dossier should always be carried in a CEO's hip pocket. To be prepared to negotiate with prospective financiers for growth and expansion capital, entrepreneurs must be in position to supply the basic financial information needed for review and evaluation on an expedited basis.

A financing dossier should contain the most common records, documents and financial disclosures that virtually any credible investor or lender would request. Savvy entrepreneurs have a financing dossier accessible and ready for circulation in quick order. They treat this document like a personal resume; everyone needs to keep one handy and keep it updated.

A guide for contents is available online through the auspices of various financing groups and institutions. Most financing institutions and private capital sources subscribe to a common list of document requirements. Standard items are listed below:

- Overview of the business model
- Summary of the relevant industry and market
- Description of core competencies or areas of specialization
- Resumes of owners and key management
- Corporate documents, including articles of incorporation, partnership agreements, and by-laws
- Company financial statements for most recent three years
- Monthly cash flow projection for two years and summary of critical assumptions underlying the projections
- Statement of proposed uses of funds
- Summary of existing business debt and copies of loan documents
- Business leases or deeds

- Description and value of collateral
- Current personal financial statements for all owners
- Current credit report for business, if available; if not, current credit reports for all owners
- Personal tax returns for prior three years for principal business owners

Sample Underwriting Guidelines

INDUSTRY PREFERENCES

Information Technology and related industries, such as Wireless Technologies

Broadband Technologies

Energy

Green Technologies

Broadcast and Media

Business Process Improvement Services

INVESTMENT STAGES

Opportunistic:

Company revenues < $1 million

Valuation < $3 million

Early stage opportunities with compelling ROI scenarios

First Stage

Proof of concept and market validation demonstrated

Achieved breakeven or profitability

Annual Revenues > $1 million

Valuation < $4 million

INVESTMENT STAGE	Second Stage Annual Revenues $3 million - $20 million Profitable enterprise Funds requested for expansion of existing markets, opening of new markets and/or acquisition of other companies
INVESTMENT SIZE	$500,000 to $2,500,000
INVESTMENT VEHICLES	Senior debt with or without equity conversion features Subordinated or mezzanine debt Participating and convertible preferred stock Common stock
GEOGRAPHIC PREFERENCES	Mid-Atlantic Region
OTHER CRITERIA	Investments made in enhancements and applications of proven technologies, not development of new technologies Demonstrated market niche Capability to scale Multiple and/or recurring revenue sources Sound business models adaptable to changes in global marketplace Strong management with proven track record Large accessible market Comprehensive and defensible financial plan Attractive valuation with favorable risk/reward profile Realistic and identifiable exit strategy[2]

In addition to developing a comprehensive dossier you must shop for prospective financiers with compatible underwriting guidelines. The criteria below is representative of the way some of the most sophisticated private lenders explain their areas of interest.

NOTABLE REFLECTIONS AT A GLANCE

- Financing alternative should be assessed strategically.
- Quantify financing needs from the start.
- Advantages and disadvantages of equity and debt should be weighed on a case-by-case basis.
- Selection of a compatible financing partner is key to a productive financing relationship.
- Lenders and investors will monitor business progress to protect funds they place at risk.
- The profile of financing needs and objectives must match the underwriting criteria of the perspective financier.
- An up-to-date financing dossier should be maintained on file.

CHAPTER NINE

Instill Peak Performace Inspect What You Expect

| *The Journey* |

BJ shared his concerns regarding Mediclean's future profitability with his accountant, Mitchell Moore and expected to receive positive feedback after discussing his plans to diversify into the technology side of the industry. Much to BJ's surprise, Mitchell was not enthusiastic.

Mitchell suggested BJ more fully analyze the causes of Mediclean's declining rate of profits before committing to this new path. He cautioned that weak financial controls could be at the root of the unfavorable earnings trend, and if so any financial dysfunctions would be compounded with diversification and growth. As such, Mitchell encouraged BJ to evaluate the quality of his company's financial checks and balances.

BJ admitted that as his business matured he had failed to closely oversee financial policies and practices such as check signing, bank deposits and cost overruns. He confessed that in recent years his priority had been sales growth. Recognizing his own shortsightedness, BJ plans to take a more active role in implementing and monitoring financial controls. He wants to start by examining controls over cash handling and cost efficiency.

Imagine, at last, your business has successfully secured long sought capital. However, despite this major triumph anxiety runs high over whether the business plan will really work. Are your projections too optimistic? Will profits fall far short of expectation? Will cash flow assumptions hold up? In the end a company's financial performance largely hinges on management precision and execution.

Just like BJ, even a well-established entrepreneur often has second thoughts about their ability to deliver on promises. Fulfillment is usually determined by how well they facilitate sales and marketing strategies as well as manage high flying expenses. For many companies, managing expenses means keeping firm grasps over labor, materials and other costs associated with finished products and services.

Achieving the goal is a daunting challenge even with a well-designed financial plan. Actual financial results could vary widely. Without coordinated financial oversight and performance, and monitoring odds for missing the mark are greatly magnified. In the final analysis, strong financial systems and safeguards are essential.

Financial oversight starts at the top of the organization. The CEO is not only the chief financial strategist but also, the chief financial inspector. For a business to achieve peak performance a strategic process must be installed and the CEO has to be fully vested to act as a watchdog. Practically speaking this means participating at some level in day-to-day oversight of operations as well as having a role in budgetary review. To steer a business toward its financial objectives its leader must set the example and get all involved accountable at some level.

It takes an extraordinary effort to mold company culture in ways that will promote best performance and strong accountability. Systems, protocols and policies have to be devised. Likewise, planned activity has to be translated into financial budgets, performance measures, and business projections.

Are you convinced your financial control and management system is sufficiently supportive to achieve your financial goals? Truth is, absent well-constructed financial systems, both productivity and profitability could be compromised without warning. With this in mind, the objective of this chapter is to highlight fundamental techniques to facilitate effective financial oversight and drive peak performance.

Chapter highlights:

- Financial Drivers
- Performance Oversight
- Budgeting and Forecasting
- Trouble Shooting
- Benchmarking

The "X" Factors

Devising a concrete set of guidelines for evaluating financial performance helps leadership decide whether its business decisions and strategies are being productive. This approach provides an objective assessment. For instance, a CEO may discover certain costs increased beyond additional revenue generated from certain products or services. This could be interpreted as meaningful sales growth but at an unacceptable rise in expenses. Likewise, a rise in high volume purchases may have qualified the business for greater price discounts and thus lowered expenses, but eaten too much free cash flow. Some of these types of well-intended actions cause major collateral damage. Therefore, a well-designed performance evaluation process not only should be holistic but take into account possible hidden trade-offs and costs.

A financial solution fit for one problem ailing a business may have side effects that give rise to another undesirable outcome. For example, eliminating billing log jams, production back-ups, employee absenteeism, unnecessary overtime pay, and chronic machine breakdowns is a goal shared by most companies. These types of conditions are generally detrimental operationally and place a heavy burden on productivity, cash flow and profitability. However, in their zeal to take corrective action management must be cautious not to implement measures so extreme they lead to could result in longer customer service response time, stock outs or increased insurance rates.

A simple comparison of your budget to actual expenses could help to identify the cause of fluctuating expenses, determine if the behavior is abnormal, and help to devise appropriate remedies. Generally speaking, budgets are adaptable and allow specific activity to be isolated as well as analyzed based on units of labor and material. To maximize performance there must be a framework for controlling profits and losses. Indeed, effective budgeting enables some companies to improve operating margins even in the face of rising operating costs. In essence, a sound budget model will help prompt a CEO discover best practices for achieving their highest profitability.

> *Inditex, the world's largest clothing retailer and parent company of Zara, can teach us much about what it means to sustain peak performance in a highly competitive industry.*
>
> *Inditex is run by entrepreneur Amancio Ortega and headquartered in Spain. Founded in 1963, the company has achieved unparalleled success with an innovative business model and extensive data collection and monitoring. Rather than hire world-class designers, Zara … politely copies them. Then it relies on a global network of shopper-feedback to tweak their designs. Corporate HQ absorbs thousands of comments and sends tweaks to their manufactures in Europe and Northern Africa, who literally sew the feedback into their next line of clothes. The clothes are shipped back, and the stock changes so quickly that shoppers are motived with a "now-or-never" choice each time they try on a blouse that won't be in-store in a few weeks. It's the user-generated approach to fast fashion.*[1]
>
> *Inditex has major brands, over 5,500 stores*[2] *and 110,000 employees. Revenue totals $17.5 billion, up approximately 50% in the last five years.*[1] *The company's net profit margin of 14.1%* [3] *is dramatically stronger than the industry average of f6.7%.*[4]
>
> *Ortega's greatest innovation is process improvement. Inditex provides a new shopping experience for customers: fast fashion at a lower price. Total vertical integration (maintaining all design and manufacturing in house rather than subcontracting these functions) and refined logistic techniques (distribution of products from manufacturing facilities to retail outlets) are among its greatest competitive strengths.*
>
> *Inditex monitors company operations extensively, ensuring progress in each step of the design and delivery systems. The bulk of its clothes are made in Spain and Morocco, close to the company's headquarters and the European market. Roughly 60% of Inditex's garments are made in company factories, while the remaining 40% of goods, usually the least time sensitive products, are outsourced.*
>
> *Company factories give the firm flexibility and speed in design and delivery. Typical turnaround time for a new design is 15 days from conception to in store – ten times faster than industry norms.*[5] *The company also maintains a relatively low inventory, by regularly feeding stores new designs rather than limiting fresh designs to once or twice per season.*
>
> *Data collection and management is a core strength of Inditex and Zara. Legend has it Ortega first used computers in analyze customer*

purchasing patterns in 1976, the year personal computers first hit the market.[6] *Today the company tracks hundreds of performance measures, from sales and inventory to items tried on but not bought and customer comments about colors and styles. Data is gathered at the local level and statistics and salesperson comments are compiled and evaluated. Stores need not sell the same items; instead, distribution is determined by local characteristics and purchase behaviors.*

Supplier performance and control has been a particular challenge for Inditex's management. Even though the company manufactures the majority of its products in house, Inditex uses approximately 1,400 suppliers. When Inditex encountered difficulties with supplier quality, reliability and working conditions, the company adopted an extensive supplier management program. Today, suppliers are required to live according to a Code of Conduct for External Manufacturers and Suppliers, and the firm audits their performance relative to product quality and efficiency, as well as employee health and safety frequently. In contrast to most apparel manufacturing arrangements, subcontracting is not permitted by Inditex.[3]

The head of IE Business School's International Entrepreneur Management Center commented on Ortega's remarkable success:

Perhaps more than any other era, today's world is in the hands of self-made men and women. Sitting at the top of the Forbes 100-wealthiest list in the United States are entrepreneurs who revolutionized the world, who changed the way that we use the telephone, listen to music, or even drink coffee. "The entrepreneur who innovates is more important; those who change the way that we do things, like Inditex's founder Amancio Ortega. And innovation is often as much about the business model as it is about using some new technological advance."[7]

There are many techniques to use to dissect operating activities tied to productivity. The key to select a design that will help both monitor and evaluate financial performance.

Poor performance trends may be indicative of bad decisions, unfavorable conditions, or a combination thereof. In the end, when it comes to sorting out problem areas an activity budget should make the job much easier.

Regular reporting is especially important so that managers and supervisors are able to keep productivity in check. The proper use of budgeting can serve to empower managers and supervisors to track their team's performance and take corrective measures when necessary. Organizations typically perform more cost effectively where staff will have financial tools like a budget to evaluate performance. The ultimate objective is get personnel throughout a company to take more ownership in budget estimates as well as performance outcomes.

Generally speaking, activity-based budgeting is adaptable for businesses engaged in fabrication, assembly and production where operations involve processing. Likewise, many fast food chains will find the approach effective in monitoring daily operations, especially where fluctuations in labor costs and inventory purchasing are closely tied to sales.

Surprisingly, activity budgeting also plays a major role in enhancing productivity in service enterprises as well. They too must overcome struggles to maximize and supervise work flow efficiency and productivity. Financial advisors generally regard activity budgeting as a prerequisite for businesses to realize a healthy bottom line.

Performance Drivers

A CEO of a growing company that spends most of his or her time in marketing but fails to notice a gaping hole in purchasing and inventory handling and processing may be setting their company up for unsatisfactory performance. Likewise, lack of focus on work flow, training and operations could result in customer delivery delays, sales returns and loss of customers.

In order to sustain long term success your key performance drivers must be in sync and working in a positive direction. You start by identifying, quantifying and continuously monitoring these components of your business. For instance, for some companies the pace of product and service innovations is the most important business driver. In other businesses a combination of sales, pricing, customer service, location and technology are paramount. These and other types of performance drivers will vary widely among business and industry.

Performance management is an ongoing process. Within a company a particular division may account for a relatively high percent of revenue but consume an escalating portion of the company's overall expenses. The source or explanation for this pattern could lead to changes in employee expense reimbursement policies, preferred vendors and other policies that influence cost factors.

Intuition alone should not be relied upon to identify where to concentrate financial controls and performance accountability. On the contrary, measurements and assessments of performance drivers should come from careful study and experimenting followed by strategic analysis. A company may benefit simply by ranking certain parts of their operation on a scale from one to ten in terms of cash flow and profit impact to ensure their time, resources and attention is being appropriately allocated. A sample illustration of a ranking grid applied to Mediclean from the case study is illustrated on the following page.

Mediclean, Inc.
Profit and Cash Flow Performance Watch List

Operational Components	Weight (1=Low Impact 15=High Impact)		
	Profit	Cash	Total
Pricing/Billing/Discounting	12	11	23
Product Mix/Sales Volume	15	15	30
Proposals/Bidding/Contract Negotiation	9	7	16
Labor Hours/Rates/Benefits	2	2	4
Staff Recruitment/Training/Retention	12	12	24
Selling Incentives/Sales Reps/Commissions	11	6	17
Locations/No. of Stores/No. of Offices	8	4	12
Advertising/Media Promotions	5	5	10
Vendor Selection/Supplier Pricing/ Credit Terms	13	9	22
Project Management/Supervision	4	4	8
Documentation/Billing/Collections	6	10	16
Intellectual Property/Licensing	3	3	6
Transportation/Shipping & Delivery	14	14	28
Technology/Systems/Communications	10	8	18
Financing Costs/Interest/Lease Rates	7	12	19

According to the ranking above the top five drivers for Mediclean in order of importance are as follows:

1. Product Mix/Sales Volume
2. Transportation/Shipping & Delivery
3. Staff Recruitment/Training/Retention
4. Pricing/Discounting
5. Vendor Selection/ Supplier Pricing/Credit Terms

Regardless of size or industry, maintaining a positive bottom line will be tied to how well financial drivers are identified, understood and managed. To keep performance in the high range, your management team must continually re-evaluate and reassess the significance of components to profits and cash flow.

Business Remodeling

As in many households, at the root of virtually every high performing business is a core set of progressive economic principles. Very often these precepts are drawn from closely aligned norms and standards exercised by successful people in everyday life. Most will agree, there are at least a dozen basic profit making principles that are universally recognized among highly achieving entrepreneurs. They speak to when, where and how to maximize business resources. The chart below features the most potent practices followed by today's most successful companies:

PRODUCTIVITY

Workflow Efficiency = High Employee Productivity

Job Training = Reduced Error Rate and Higher Output

Equipment Upgrade or Replacement = Less Downtime and Increased Production

Temporary Labor = Avoid Disruption and Maintain Output Levels

COST CONTROL

Periodic Inventories = Improved Accountability and Asset Protection

Waste Controls and Recycling = Lower Unit Cost

Shipping & Storage = Lower Carrier and Space Cost

Quality Management = Minimizes Customer Returns

Outsourcing = Cost Savings

PROFIT AND CASH FLOW

Sales Growth = Higher Income and Added Cash Flow

Production Unit Costing = Profit Margin Control and Management

Receivables Collection = Accelerated Cash Flow and Lower Level of Financing

Spending Limits = Built-In Spending Control

Financial Audit = Heightened Financial Compliance and Objectivity

Too often, businesses neglect to think about or explore these fundamental percepts before formulating their system of performance management and oversight.

Even when a business is convinced that its performance results are spectacular, it never hurts to compare these numbers to those of other industry leaders. In this regard, growing number of companies rely on a relatively simple method known as "benchmarking" to guard against complacency and stagnation. This technique basically gathers for comparison, the best information available from as many credible sources as possible, both within and outside the business. Then, the methods used by compatible high achievers are systematically implemented.

Benchmarking helps erase the false assumption that operational performance is ideal. On contrary, the method of performance evaluation relies extensively on outside external comparisons to validate internal assumptions. For instance, a retail business may decide to set benchmarks based on companies that achieve superior in-store sales at minimum cost; or which are widely known for exceptional customer satisfaction. These companies may be inclined to look to Apple Computers and Trader Joe's:

Apple's retail stores recently reported annual revenue per square foot of over $6,000 exceeds that if such notable stores as Lululemon, Neiman Marcus and Coach.[1] Red Herring defined Apple's recipe for success:

Unlike its rivals, Apple gives customers instant gratification by keeping inventory in stores. The company has opened stores slowly, building up anticipation for its stores. Their stores are some of the tiniest in retail – encouraging customers to drop far more money than they might in a dusty computer shop or utilitarian web site. [1]

Trader Joe's is widely acclaimed for its customer friendly focus. Fast Company summarizes the company's approach.

Trader Joe's business model allows it to respond to customer feedback in ways that other supermarkets cannot. Suppliers do not pay fees, or "rent," to place products on Trader Joe's shelves, a widespread industry practice that's anything but customer-focused. With drastically smaller square footage and inventories than typical grocery stores, the company removes items that don't sell well to make room for new products. In a sense, Trader Joe's entire inventory is a result of listening to customers – both their feedback and their dollars.[2]

Benchmarking is not only germane to retail merchandising and manufacturing but also for service enterprises. To remain competitive and highly responsive to evolving customer expectations and purchasing trends the service industry in general is trending toward a greater reliance on benchmarking.

For service businesses of nearly every stripe, particularly in North America and Europe, manufacturing provides a glimpse into the future. Under unrelenting competitive pressure, they are reexamining the role of operations in creating competitive advantage and asking themselves which clearly differentiated services they can provide and how they can deliver those services to customers as efficiently as possible – and more effectively than their rivals do. Today's leading industrial companies asked and answered similar questions two decades ago, and many executives of service companies now believe that they can adopt the methodologies and tools that have already transformed manufacturers. [3]

In search for the most innovate ways to spark business performance among service enterprises, a management-board member of AXA Insurance Company stated, "We are using approaches that have worked very effectively at manufacturing companies and adapting them to our environment. These approaches include... benchmarking costs among AXA companies."[4] When it comes to best practices it is not always necessary to reinvent the wheel. Many techniques employed by very successful companies are available in the public domain for use in formulating better business practices.

Parts Unknown

Many people in business confess boredom, if not apathy, at the need to link superior financial performance analysis to a daily business oversight routine. The tendency among many leaders is to marginalize and undervalue the day to day analytical process and its significance to the bottom line. On the contrary, a detailed analysis of daily activities related to sales, labor and material costs is usually a prerequisite for growing profits on a consistent basis.

Your daily review and assessment of financial data gives monthly and annual forecasts and budgets credence and reliability. Although forecasts should not be wedded to past performance, history is sometimes the most reliable foundation to predict the future. Past experience can be most reliable in terms of mapping out future expenses for personnel, equipment and supplies. Many times, the advantage that one business enjoys over another rests solely with superior methods of financial review, planning and forecasting. Companies that master oversight tends to succeed not only based on competitive pricing but efficiency as well.

Forecasting is also essential in smoothing work flow. A well planned production forecast also can serve as a dependable guidepost for estimating future financial expenditures. In business, effective management of resources hinges on making decisions tied to these estimates. A blueprint developed in each area advance drives the efficient deployment of resources.

With less room for error, for many small businesses, it is especially important to synchronize sales and expense forecasts monthly, quarterly, as well as annually. Without a periodic point of reference it could be difficult to recognize budget deviations in time to take corrective action. Absent a protocol, a business could overlook spikes in purchase prices of raw material, merchandise, and outside services to its demise.

Sound forecasting is indeed the backbone of a performance driven enterprise. Whether a business is centralized or decentralized, a tightly knitted forecasting technique is invaluable. These techniques contribute to improving operating systems by instilling discipline and promoting accountability throughout all company divisions and departments. A reliable production forecasting model could also serve as a criteria to set bonus or incentive compensation for managers and supervisors.

A chief decision-maker, CEO or President should never make the mistake of assuming the responsibility for financial oversight falls strictly in their accountant's domain. Whether choosing the key performance drivers, selecting budget line items to track more closely or creating lines of accountability leadership should always be intricately engaged.

Trouble-Shooting Made Easy

Many companies rely heavily on their budgeting and reporting system to spot trouble early enough to prevent irreparable damage to their bottom-line. When a budget is closely scrutinized, attention will most likely be drawn to unexplained variations. A budget vs actual comparisons may consist of a three columnar presentation: budget, actual, and variance. A "variance" will be a reflection of the magnitude to which your business tactics and strategies were positive or negative.

The key to effective trouble shooting is not only identifying significant budget deviations but scrutinizing key assumptions underlying each budget line item. Because of the need to perform a "look back," key assumptions should always be listed in writing in an attachment to the budget. This will enable each operating division, department and staff person to be in position to look back and determine how and why things may have gone wrong.

It is also helpful analytically when line items in the financial budget mirror the chart of accounts used for financial statement purposes. The chart of accounts is a descriptive list of account titles used for accumulating financial activity to be reported in the financial statements. Ideally, it should be relatively easy to compare budgets and financial statements using the following measurements:

- Line item expense as a percent of revenues
- Net income as a percent of gross sales

- Labor hours in comparison to production
- Cost of goods as percent of gross sales
- Sales potential based on production

A streamline illustration of a financial budget for Matrix featuring the qualities described is presented below:

A quick glance of the illustrative budget report for MediClean provides a view of major variances between budget and actual performance.

Mediclean, Inc. Financial Budget ($000 Omitted)

	Actual	Budget	Variance
Revenues			
Cleaning Products	$10,500	$11,250	-750
Dining Room Products	26,000	23,750	2,250
Total Revenues	36,500	35,000	1,500
Cost of Goods Sold			
Cleaning Products	$7,350	$6,950	($400)
Dining Room Products	16,900	16,000	-900
Total Cost of Goods Sold	24,250	22,950	-1300
Gross Profit	$12,250	$12,050	$200
Selling and Operating Expenses	10,420	10,000	-420
Net Income (Loss)	$1,830	$2,050	($220)

- Sales of cleaning products were $750,000 under budget, while dining room products were $2,250,000 ahead of projection.
- For dining room products, inventory purchases classified as "cost of goods sold" exceeded budget by $900,000, and the cleaning products division was also over budget by $400,000.
- Overall net income (gross profit less selling and operating expenses) was $220,000 unfavorable compared to budget.
- A progressive management team would be inclined to investigate and analyze the favorable or unfavorable reasons behind the differences shown.

Performance Outliers

Business earnings sometimes become anemic due to unforeseen events. In other words, the bottom line is subject to be favorably or adversely affected by performance outliers. They may involve passage of new regulations, lawsuits employee turnover and other circumstances outside the control of management. Without a fined tuned method of analyzing variances such financial performance these types of occurrences could mistakenly be attributed to operational shortcomings.

A simple financial analysis can be demonstrated by reference to the Mediclean case study. A main cost area that prevented the company from maximizing earnings was cost of goods. The maintenance division was unfavorable by $400,000. To get to the underlying causes, the following analysis of usage and price could be performed.

MEDICLEAN, INC. VARIANCE ANALYSIS

	Budget Price	Budget Quantity	Combined Total
MAINTENANCE:			
Cleaning Detergent - Budget	$5.00 / gal.	1,390,000 gals.	$6,950,000
Price Variance:			
Actual Price	$5.00 / gal.		
-- Budgeted Price	$4.75/ gal.		
Difference	$0.25 / gal.		
x Budgeted Quantity	1,390,000 gals		
Price Variance - Unfavorable	$347,500		
Volume Variance:			
Actual Quantity		1,400,500 gals.	
- Budgeted Quantity		1,390,000 gals.	
Difference		10,500 gals.	
x Budgeted Price		$5 / gal.	
Volume (usage) Variance - Unfavorable		$52,500	
Recap of Total Budget Variance:		$347,500	
Price Variance			
Volume Variance		52,500	
400,000			
Actual Cost of Goods Sold			$7,350,000

The results of evaluation above indicates that Mediclean experienced a significant budget variance in cost of goods sold attributed to an unfavorable price reduction of $.25 per gallon totaling in aggregate, $347,500. Likewise, the usage of detergent was over budget by 10,400 gallons resulting in $52,500 unfavorable variance. A combination of the two overages resulted in a $400,000 unfavorable variance.

As the CEO of Mediclean, you might ask: "Was the price increase avoidable by switching suppliers; or was the use of detergents wasteful?" In the final analysis, you would want to determine whether the overages were within the control of your managers and supervisors. A general guide for determining the influence of price and usage variances is provided below.

Price Variance = (Actual Price – Budget Price) x Budgeted Volume

> *Measures the variance in revenues or expenses resulting from the difference between the budgeted average price per unit sold or purchased and the realized actual price.*

Volume Variance = (Actual Volume – Budget Volume) x Budgeted Price

> *Measures the variance in revenues or expenses resulting from the difference between the budgeted and the realized volume of activity.*

Notable Reflections at a Glance

- Budget anticipated expenditure of funds associated with producing products or rendering services.
- Take time to translate assigned performance expectations to various operating units, departments and staff.

CHAPTER TEN

Tighten Up Legally... Lockdown Prosperity

| *The Journey* |

After much deliberation, BJ has concluded diversification would be the most effective way to protect market share and profits in the future. Convinced the best opportunity for growth could be in customizing technology solutions for inventory control and distribution, he decides to launch a new technology venture.

Nevertheless, ambition did not cloud his sense of reasoning. BJ felt he would not be the ideal person to manage technical operations within an IT company. Consequently, he asked his good friend Taylor who has the technical expertise to consider teaming up, and to his great pleasure, Taylor responded enthusiastically to the overture.

The friends recognized that many decisions had been made regarding their business relationship from the outset of their discussion. However, they still must agree upon the type of legal entity. Alternatives include a joint venture, merger or subcontracting relationship. Taylor opposed forming a corporation, in favor of a limited liability company and BJ, less concerned about choice of entity was eager to decide their respective investment contribution and share of profit and loss.

> The pair agreed $300,000 was the magic number necessary to mobilize operations. They anticipate the bulk of funds will be used for start up costs, including working capital, marketing and business development. The remainder will be necessary to purchase various computer equipment, accessories, and software.
>
> To Taylor's chagrin, BJ also insisted on a buy-sell agreement. He felt it would be invaluable, should either he or Taylor need to withdraw from the business due to disability, death, or personal reasons.

If you are like most entrepreneurs, when you started or expanded your business you rushed into a legal structure without fully understanding the legal distinctions among the various choices. Many times, selecting one legal form over another is solely based on tidbits from friends, colleagues and TV commercials rather than on the sound advice of a CPA or business attorney.

The prospect for legal liability in excess of business insurance coverage poses a serious enough threat and gets every business owner's attention. The party who wins in a lawsuit and awarded money damages is referred to as a judgment creditor. Judgment creditors usually look to be paid either from the debtor's insurance or by legally seizing and selling the debtor's business assets. Afterwards, if the judgment is still not completely satisfied they may turn to the personal assets of business owner to the extent they may be legally accessible.

Just focusing on making a profit without regard to various legal means for asset protection would be a big mistake for any business owner or investor. A key to keeping a business financially stable is protecting the legal interest of its stakeholders. For good reason, shareholders and owners want to be shielded from personal liability.

Unless the friends and colleagues who advised you early on were business lawyers, a fresh evaluation of your choice of legal entity is probably in order. To this end, this chapter provides some basic guidance and considerations to get you started.

CHAPTER HIGHLIGHTS:

- Asset Protection
- Choice of Business Entity
- Teaming Alternatives
- Buy-Sell Arrangements
- Proactive Legal Practices

Clipping Legal Hassles

One of the most important steps in establishing a business is the selection of a form of incorporation. Even when an established businesses decides to form an unrelated or distinct new line of product or service it is wise to consider forming another legal entity. By custom, many larger businesses establish multiple companies or affiliates. New spin offs may be comprised of several subsidiaries legally separate but affiliated by common ownership. One reason to carve up a business into separate legal parts is to shield the business assets of the parent. The goal is to keep a profit making parent protected legally from financial losses or failure of a new start-up operation.

As a practical matter, investors in a flagship venture may not be interested in assuming any financial risk associated with an unrelated business or new business pursuit. In order to make all parties happy, a new separate company could be created. Understandably, while hoping to maximize return on investment most business owners and shareholders are relunctant to expose their residence, personal savings, investment property, securities and other assets to debts of a business. Rather, to the extent possible stakeholders generally strive to restrict any personal exposure for legal damages to recovery against their financial investment.

Preserving precious intangible business assets also precipitates construct of a multitier corporate structure. This is especially true where the plight of a start-up operation could place a parent's well established goodwill, reputation and brand name in jeopardy. Once again, incorporating another separate legal entity could be a remedy.

Likewise, in the context of a teaming relationship each group of business owners may prefer to utilize a separate legal affiliate to house their partnership. In fact, it is common for a joint venture to be established with a written agreement and through of a separate legal entity to enable the planned project or specific contract to be administered without directly involving each partner's primary business.

Limiting Investor Liability

For the most part, incorporating is one of the most effective ways to provide owners and investors the all-important advantage of "limited personal legal liability." This construct generally limits investor exposure to creditor debts and legal judgments to their financial investment in the enterprise. From a strategic perspective there are a variety of ways even this conventional form of protection may be tested.

In legal battles where a business is named as a defendant, an aggrieved party may argue in court that an entity's "corporate veil" should be pierced. If the argument holds up, the aggrieved party could chase after the business owner and any other investors personally to recover any legal damages awarded by the courts. Piercing the corporate veil would most likely be pursued when the losing party lacks sufficient resources to pay a judgment. The plaintiff might ask the court to unveil the legal cloak of protection if they have evidence the defendant actually operated like a "mom and pop" business where liabilities of person and business were legally intertwined.

When personal and business funds flow through the same bank account courts are more inclined to find that owner and business acted as a single unit and not as separate entities.

On the other hand, courts tend to dismiss pleas to pierce the corporate veil especially when an incorporated business and its owners are able to demonstrate proper legal practices and protocols have been followed on a consistent basis. The opposite is true when owners commingle their personal and business finances. When personal and business funds flow through the same bank account courts are more inclined to find that owner and business acted as a single unit and not as separate entities. For this reason, combining cash deposits and disbursements in a single bank account is a "no no."

When circumstances give rise for courts to weigh the possibility of lifting the corporate veil of protection owners and investors could be vulnerable legally. The best legal defense may rest in demonstrating the business conformed to mandatory corporate operating requirements. It also pays for business owners to be very familiar with the aforementioned basic do's and don'ts related to how incorporated businesses should be managed procedurally and financially.

Whether a corporation is large or small most state jurisdictions stipulate how often, if it all, they must conduct annual meetings of the shareholders and directors. In between formal annual meetings a special meeting or voting process could be mandated for extraordinary decisions involving merger, consolidation, or sale of substantially all business assets. These qualifications make a compelling case for retaining a business attorney throughout the life cycle of a business.

Looming Legal Hazards

To bring stark reality to the hazards of personal liability consider this straight forward hypothetical. A friend of yours establishes a wholesale distribution business as a sole proprietorship with an investment of $40,000. Anxious to gain a major new customer, she accepts a sales order within the first week.

Two months afterwards, the wheels start to come off. Your friend's company was unable to deliver the product. Unfortunately, because the overseas manufacturer got behind schedule due to a production backlog. This whole predicament left your friend in a "Catch 22," both unable to meet the demands of the customer and unable to force the supplier to deliver.

Assume there was no written agreement specifying conditions of performance and that your friend's business was unincorporated. In the worst case scenario customer is awarded legal damages of $100,000. As demonstrated in the chart on the following page, your friend's personal net worth would be tapped to the tune of $60,000 in the absence of incorporation. Her personal net worth would drop from $200K to $140K. Suffice it to say, the legal perils of faulty legal handiwork far outweigh the cost of diligent coverage.

A sound legal structure takes on even higher degree of significance in certain industries that are inherently dangerous. Companies at the high end of this risk curve include demolition, excavation and construction businesses. However, even in industries that might otherwise appear to be least at risk, dangers of liability lurk. Claims for wrongful employee discharge, negligence, and breach of contract are just a few of the types of employer liabilities that can crop up.

Litigation risks vary from one business to another, but be assured all businesses operate at some level of exposure. Accordingly, proper legal formation and maintenance of a business organization should be a high priority.

Advice for Newborns

When establishing a new venture or separating a division into a distinct company, a choice must be made regarding the type of incorporation. This decision could have far reaching implications. Conceivably, possible ramifications stretch from roles and responsibilities of owners and officers to how legal ownership is legally transferrable. Legal forms of business organization also have decidedly different consequences for income tax purposes. With these types of considerations in mind, a final determination of legal form should only be made with proper guidance from your CPA and team of legal advisors.

For the most part, state laws make it relatively straight forward for businesses of all sizes to be incorporated. The basic options made available include a limited liability company or corporation. In most states LLCs or corporations can be selected for single-owner as well as multiple owner business ventures. Therefore, a budding one person owned businesses need never rule out incorporation.

Generally speaking, the corporate form of business is most suitable for a venture with numerous investors where frequent exchanges and transfers of ownership are anticipated. The corporate structure promotes centralized management wherein, control is mostly exercised by a few on behalf of many. Corporate directors normally fulfill this role and oversee the business from a policy perspective. Directors are also responsible for appointing officers to manage day-to-day business affairs.

In large part, the operating template for a corporation is provided by law. Most state laws set specific procedures and legal boundaries with respect to voting rights of shareholders, the board of directors and executive officers. Regulations even prescribe the frequency of shareholder and board meetings.

For the most part, state laws make it relatively straight forward for businesses of all sizes to be incorporated.

On the other hand, a LLC or Limited Liability Company model is a viable and, some believe less cumbersome, than the corporate model. In general, a limited liability company

(LLC) works best when a company has a smaller number of owners and investors. State LLC regulations tend to be more flexible than their corporate counterpart in terms of standard procedures and protocols. For example, through an operating agreement owners or members of limited liability companies are allowed to customize their business relationships in terms of distribution of ownership, method of sharing of profits and losses and division of management authority. The desires and needs of owners and best captured in a written document.

Start-ups are not alone in the quest to find a compatible legal form of business. After careful analysis mature businesses often rediscover reasons to change or convert their legal entity of choice. These moves could be prompted by changes in ownership or new tax laws. Even in the absence of such developments, it is wise to re-evaluate your legal entity at least once every three years.

The Slippery Slope

Once duly incorporated a surprising number of entrepreneurs fail to keep their business in "good standing." When this occurs the legal status must be revived otherwise many of the legal protections previously described could be lost. One might ask, how an entrepreneur would allow their business to forfeit limited liability protection? Many times, a lapse in legal status comes by way of default for failure to file tax returns or other periodic procedural filing requirement.

When administration and communication breakdown, an entrepreneur may haphazardly discover their default status long after the fact. For instance, failure to renew a business license or pay annual state and local taxes may be required by statute however, notices and reminders are not always provided. This places the onus on the business to keep track. Technically, when the legal status is in default the business could be found to legally have reverted to a sole proprietorship and general partnerships and have no limited liability protection.

Likewise, a sole proprietorship and general partnership could be deemed to exist legally based on the conduct of the people involved. Under common law, a person or persons who pursue an activity for profit could be deemed legally to be operating business. This could be a major shock to someone who never explicitly agreed to form a business relationship.

Consequently, whenever you associate with others for the purpose of generating income it pays to seek competent legal counsel.

Ties That Bind

Many businesses discover the most economical and strategic way to grow market share is through teaming or partnering with another company. For many early stage and mature businesses this strategy has proven to be highly effective for purposes of igniting growth and higher profits. Benefits could stem from an accelerated sales growth, greater chance to secure financing, or spreading cost of overhead over a much larger customer base. Many Fortune 500 companies routinely search for opportunities to acquire companies with a wide distribution channel, substantial customer base or specialized technology.

Despite the attraction, it would be unwise to form a team without a written agreement. Needless to say, verbal arrangements are highly susceptible to misinterpretation and could become the source of protracted and costly litigation. It is best for a teaming relationship to be well-documented. Furthermore, defining the key parameters of the association adds value and substance to the relationship.

Under certain circumstances it may be advantageous for long-time competitors or suppliers to consider joining forces. Collectively they command a much larger market share. Partnering also makes sense when one party possesses excess operating or technical capacity. This could also help eliminate duplicate administrative and overhead expenses. In the end, forming a teaming relationship more may be economical and cost effective for both companies.

Some of the most common templates for teaming include the following:

JOINT VENTURE

A joint venture is a legal business association between two or more companies. Usually this type of association is narrowly defined to cover a specific business opportunity or undertaking. The joint venture agreement sets terms and conditions of the business relationship in terms of capital investment requirements, duration, and split of profit and loss. Stipulations regarding management authority and the decision making process are also spelled out.

MERGER OR CONSOLIDATION

A merger or consolidation between two companies is generally much more legally encompassing than a joint venture. In essence, a merger or consideration is the equivalent of a full blown marriage between two separate businesses. From a legal perspective, one or both of the businesses involved will lose its identity and become a single entity legally and financially. Assets, liabilities, ownership rights and obligations are pooled under one roof.

SUBCONTRACTING

Subcontracting is probably the most common way to create a teaming relationship. Typically subcontracting is involved when one company decides to hire another to perform specific work requirements for a customer. As opposed to a joint venture or merger there is no sharing of risks and rewards. In most cases the subcontractor usually simply agrees to complete the assigned work for a specific price. The prime contractor is no more than a broker.

Selecting a compatible teaming model is the equivalent of selecting a legal entity. In both cases, care should be exercised and professional legal advice should be sought.

Sweet Harmony

Without a comprehensive agreement among and between owners and investors most businesses would be susceptible to abrupt breakups and internal battles. Too often, private businesses dissolve due to internal strife that could have been avoided. Too often owners fail to take time from the outset to draft a written agreement covering their business relationship. At great risk legally, founding members often rely solely on trust. Naively, they believe their mutual admiration, respect and friendship will endure no matter what. Unfortunately, history has shown otherwise.

The best way to head off legal turmoil is with a basic written contract between the owners. Owner contracts are often referred to as shareholders' agreements, operating agreements and buy-sell agreements. In small privately owned companies they promote harmony by spelling out the rules of the game as agreed to in advance.

Regardless of your personal beliefs and confidence in colleagues it would be unwise to dismiss the possibility of future misunderstanding, hostility, or animosity. Indeed many experienced business people believe it is best for owner agreements to be drawn up before the first day of business. A buy-sell arrangement could take the form of a stand alone contract or be merged as part of a corporation's shareholder agreement. On the other hand, for limited liability companies is common to insert a buy-sell provision in the Operating Agreement.

When carefully and thoughtfully drafted, an agreement between the owners should leave very little room for controversy should they ever decide to part ways. The agreement provides essential guidance in case of separation or dissolution for both voluntary and involuntary reasons.

...for limited liability companies is common to insert a buy-sell provision in the Operating Agreement.

Another pivotal part of a buy-sell provision is the valuation clause. Invariably upon departure, whether voluntary or not, each owner will expect fair remuneration. The problem arises when there is a variation in views about what amount constitutes a fair value.

A variety of legitimate valuation questions may arise concerning various tangible and intangible assets held by a business. The most highly debatable values surround goodwill, customer lists, trademarks and copyrights, as well as hard assets including equipment and real estate. In the absence of a prescribed valuation approach different methods could produce results that vary widely.

It is extremely important for the owners of a company to agree in advance on a specific valuation approach. Valuation methods in buy-sell agreements usually differ from value determinations performed for bank loan purposes. For the most part business valuations for buy-sell purposes are typically determined by agreed fixed price, appraisal process or predetermined formula.

A brief short survey of the most basic methods are as follows:

Net Book Value – Value is derived from equity reported on the balance sheet of the business.

Fair Market Value – Appraised value of net assets ordinarily set by outside appraisal or other professional assessor.

Formula – Prescribed formulas use average current and past net earnings adjusted for good will and any other intangibles.

It behooves entrepreneurs to seek advice from their team of professional advisors before deciding on an appropriate valuation approach.

After deciding on a valuation approach business owners should carefully consider how a buyout provision will actually be funded. Buy-sells are sometimes funded through life insurance in case of death or outright cash purchase in other situations. Alternatively, a payment plan in the form of a promissory note may be used. The latter could avoid the necessity for the remaining business owners to sell off operating assets just to generate the dollars to purchase the withdrawing owner's interest.

Business Planning Ins & Outs

In the end, the silver lining beneath the marketing façade of most long standing businesses, is a tightly knitted business structure. Lack of legal structure need not be a weakness among many entrepreneurial companies. On the contrary, a solid legal structure serves not only to shield business creditors but clarify rights and duties of ownership. In essence, a well-crafted legal framework specifies rights, privileges and duties of its equity investors. Greater cohesion usually exist because these relationships are spelled out in writing. They are guided by Bylaws, Operating and Shareholder's Agreements.

Some of the more fundamental privileges, duties and rights typically be addressed as part of the legal planning process include the following:

- Voting Terms and Conditions
- Officer Designations and Responsibilities
- Stock Transfer Restrictions Rights, if any
- Admission to Ownership
- Compensation of Owners, if any
- Life Insurance on Key Officers
- Term of Business (i.e., Limited or Perpetual)

Other basic areas of legal governance and administration that also may be required include:

- Annual Meetings
- Special Meetings
- Place of Meetings
- Notice of Meetings
- Quorum
- Conduct and Location of Meetings

When owners regularly revisit these pivotal areas the risk of business break up over trivial issues of personality and discretion is much lower.

Finally, in some instances state statutes and regulations will dictate certain corporate governance rules and practices. Notable areas subject to variation in different jurisdictions include:

Sample Corporate Governance Rules and Practices *Subject to Variation by Jurisdiction*

	Corporations	LLCs
Management Roles and Responsibilities	The board of directors appoints officers to be responsible for management of specific divisions, including President/CEO (Chief Executive Officer); Vice President/COO (Chief Operating Officer); Controller/CFO (Chief Financial Officer). The board also designates the scope of specific duties and responsibilities for each officer in the bylaws. This structure provides a ready chain of command. The Board of Directors is elected by the owner/shareholders of the corporation.	Owners, referred to as "Members," may elect to manage the affairs of the business collectively, appoint a member designated as the Manager, hire a non-member Manager, or create a structure with officers inclusive of President/CEO (Chief Operating Officer), and other officer positions.
Distribution of Profits and Loses	Ordinarily dividends have to be authorized by a majority of the board of directors or shareholders. Dividends normally are paid based on the number and class of stock shares held. Shareholders also can be compensated as employees for services rendered.	LLCs generally have discretion to decide how profits and losses will be allocated among members subject to special tax law regulations. Tiers of profit distribution may be agreed upon by the members. Members also may agree to make guaranteed payments as compensation to members for services rendered.

Sample Corporate Governance Rules and Practices *Subject to Variation by Jurisdiction*

	Corporations	LLCs
CAPITAL INVESTMENT	Depending on jurisdiction eligible Close Corporations with a shareholder agreement can determine the maximum capital investment of shareholders. Otherwise corporate law in the jurisdiction controls rights over purchase of new stock shares.	By agreement members usually are allowed to specify minimum or maximum capital investment amounts; or provide voting discretion by majority to decide whether to invest additional capital. Most states permit the Operating Agreement to state applicable criteria.
ADMISSION OF NEW OWNER	Generally there is no limit on the number of shareholders unless otherwise stated in a governing document such as a Shareholder's Agreement. Majority of board or shareholders approve new stock issues. This is an ideal model for businesses with numerous investors or that plan to raise capital publicly as in an initial public offering (IPO).	Members generally are allowed to establish and/or vote on criteria for admission of a new member. Otherwise, consistent with laws of the jurisdiction the Operating Agreement usually establishes a maximum limit on the number of people who may become members.

CHAPTER ELEVEN

Downsize Business Risks... Guard the Upside

| *The Journey* |

After agreeing on a legal structure, the business associates turned to carefully evaluate the worst case. BJ reminded Taylor how businesses stand to take a nosedive due to unexpected personal tragedies affecting its founders. Likewise, many businesses plummet after being victimized by a major natural disaster.

Taylor suggested a visit to a financial professional to work out plans for coverage in the event of death or disability of either party. She also suggested reexamining back up data file and information security protocols along with a disaster recovery plan.

In turn BJ recommended they formulate a succession strategy or plan to sell the business in the future should the circumstances warrant. He noted for instance, in the event they did not identify someone to take over such as a family member they should be in position to put the business on the market.

Taylor liked the idea of having a succession plan but felt increasing the value of their investment should be their first priority. In the end, she too hoped for a large capital gain down the road.

> To make certain they do not overlook any other critical concerns, BJ suggested they form an advisory board or board of directors to help govern the new venture. He credits much of Mediclean's success to the advice he received from his board. He believes the new venture could be well served by following the same practice.

Finally, your business is in full swing with steady sales growth, increasing profits, positive cash flow, and ample financing. Your dreams are coming true and you are flying high. Are you home free? Not just yet.

Even with a well-crafted legal structure you have to take steps to manage and reduce inherent operating risks. Otherwise, your company will be at high risk to collapse financially. Most business veterans agree, the question is not whether or not a business owner will confront a potentially devastating occurrence or set of circumstances but whether they have built mechanisms to withstand the shock?

After working tirelessly to build a financially sound business, carelessly leaving it exposed to loss of investment would be foolish. Yet, this possibility arises whenever you fail to identify and work to mitigate the most significant enterprise risks. At the root, the focus of enterprise risks is any inherently plausible events that could prove deadly to the survival of the business.

If you are like most entrepreneurs your worst fears could include any of the following…

- Your right hand person—the only employee trained to function at a management level—suddenly and unexpectedly resigns.
- Due to your own illness you are forced to take a leave of absence for several months or more.
- A major customer constituting a sizable portion of your business revenues files bankruptcy.
- Your handpicked successor is unable to continue their duties due to disability.
- Under the buy-sell agreement a departing owner is entitled to a payment of $300,000, however, cash in the bank and from other sources only approximates $100,000.

- Your principle business office is hit by a hurricane destroying vital business information such as customer sales, accounts receivable and disabling computer systems.

Entrepreneurs are confronted with these and other high risk concerns everyday. In this chapter my focus will be you start a process to risk assessment, evaluation and mitigation.

CHAPTER HIGHLIGHTS:

- Income Protection
- Safety Measures
- Business Valuation
- Managing Risks
- Exit Strategies
- Damage Controls

Wise Risk Management

It would be naïve, and some might argue irresponsible to ignore risks associated with every day life. In this respect, most people consider it wise to think through both best and worst case scenarios involving personal harm or possible human loss and to take reasonable precautions through insurance and other forms of protection.

Similarly, loss of a business owner, CEO or key officer could be the last nail in the coffin of any business enterprise especially a small one. Indeed, any type of significant personal set back to any key person could trigger a major domino effect not only impacting the company but its employees and their families as well. For this reason risk management should be at the top of a CEO's agenda. Like other pivotal matters that have to be confronted in managing the life of a business, effective risk management requires careful planning and execution. There may be no single way or answer when it comes to mitigating all significant risks. Nevertheless, the effort has the potential to be very fruitful.

One widespread and highly accredited approach to mitigation is known as enterprise risk management. Enterprise risk management has been adopted by many large companies and organizations to both identify, qualify and manage significant business risks. The goal of the model is to prompt organizations in systematically examining risks inherent to their particular business, industry and environment. Because these are universal concerns enterprise risk management has been a failsafe for large organizations as well as mid-size and small companies.

Like their large counterparts smaller businesses face a variety of strategic and operating risks that have the potential to derail their stability. The range of concerns stretch from litigation, regulatory violations and assessed penalties to loss of major customer, cancellation of bank financing and loss of key personnel. Any business that fails to devise ways to effectively manage such risks is highly vulnerable.

Any business that fails to devise ways to effectively manage such risks is highly vulnerable.

In order to implement an enterprise risk management strategy you first have to undertake a process of research, evaluation and strategic planning. The research and analysis is critical to ensure that the most crucial type of risks specific to your company will be identified. On the other hand, the evaluation phase attempts to measure potential damage and search out mitigation risk solutions. The assessment may require the assistance of outside professionals or consultants.

Lastly, the strategic planning phase of risk analysis should entail ranking risks is according to likelihood of occurrence and potential impact level. A plant must then be devised to assign responsibility for monitoring and coordinating risk mitigation protocols to particular managers or units within the business.

With the precepts of enterprise risk management in mind, several universal risk concerns common to most companies will be considered in this chapter.

Personal Backstops

It is well known today that a substantial number of home foreclosures are tied to personal setbacks stemming from accidental personal injuries and chronic illnesses. These situations can lead to personal bankruptcy as well as the demise of your business enterprise where there is a gap in insurance. Accordingly, many businesses should not only strive to carry adequate commercial liability insurance but sufficient health, disability and life insurance for its employees and especially key executives.

Among the major concerns for virtually every Company is the physical well-being of their company's key personnel. The concern is magnified with respect to a small company that heavily relies on the business owner to for day-to-day management. Suffice it to say, ample insurance coverage for key personnel and other employees is critical for any business to survive over the long term. Likewise, healthy work force will usually enjoy lower absenteeism, higher productivity and better morale.

In many small companies, personal and business legal and financial obligations become intertwined; and virtually inseparable. A set back on either the business or personal side could jeopardize the vitality of the entire business enterprise.

Viability is tenuous. A company's ability to repay a business loan may be highly dependent on the good health of the owner or other key personnel to enable their day to day active participation. Likewise, the well-being of certain employees can affect the company's ability to follow through on short and long term plans and commitments.

Disability insurance is another vital form of insurance protection. Disability insurance most often serves to replace lost wages when an insured is unable to work due to a work or non-work related disability. Just as their employees, most business owners are dependent on income from their company to maintain their standard of living. In the event of a long-term absence, disability insurance benefits could avoid the potential depletion of the firm's cash by the owner who may otherwise divert resources in an attempt to support their personal financial needs.

Typically, disability plans cover 60% to 70% of pre-tax earnings ninety days after becoming disabled. Your insurance professional can advise you on other important features regulating policy renewal and cancellation, inflation protection, rehabilitation assistance, and waiting periods.

Because expensive nursing and physical rehabilitation services are unaffordable for most people over the long term, long-term care insurance is also essential. Unfortunately, too often long-term care insurance is often overlooked by business owners when devising comprehensive risk management plan. Aside from health insurance, long-term care insurance is arguably the next most important. Usually, long-term care insurance coverage provides reimbursement for extended long term-care, including nursing stays and home care services. Premiums for long-term care insurance vary depending on age, deductible period, years of coverage, inflation protection and other options. Regardless of age, prudent financial planning requires consideration of long-term care.

Long-term care pays a vital role in risk protection. Most people simply could not afford to pay out of pocket costs for long-term care costs in the event of a catastrophic or prolonged illness. Just the cost of nursing care alone could financially wipe out the average person. Needless to say, government assistance may not be an option especially with the added burden of the expenses of a business. Consequently, the simple solution may be long-term health care insurance. At a minimum, long-term care insurance could help to prevent personal bankruptcy and preserve one's personal net worth.

If a company becomes obligated to repurchase stock due to death of key owner, the proceeds from insurance could be the source of funding.

Another critical prong in any strategic risk management plan is life insurance. One of the most important life insurance decisions for business owners is determining the amount of necessary coverage. From a business perspective, the appropriate level of coverage depends on whether the policy is designed to fund buyout or provide recovery money for the business. The distinction can make a huge difference in selecting the amount of coverage. Moreover, life insurance can be an effective substitute and replacement for building cash reserves needed to fulfill personal and business commitments in the event of an entrepreneurs' death.

It also is a common practice for companies to take out life insurance as a hedge against death of key personnel such as its CEO or president. In this event, the proceeds from insurance would be available to help support the company financially during a costly transition as well as defray expenses for services of an executive search firm. Likewise, life insurance may be tied to buy-sell agreements. If a company becomes obligated to repurchase stock due to death of key owner, the proceeds from insurance could be the source of funding. In the absence of the special types of insurance coverage discussed, a company may lack the financial means to fulfill promises.

Deciding precisely how much insurance coverage is an appropriate question to work through and is a matter that should be in consultation with your insurance and other professional advisors. Naturally, this decision usually varies on an individual basis. In any case, the goal should be to align an insurance protection to accommodate and provide a cushion to you and your family in the event a life changing circumstance does in fact occur.

Funny Money

Some type of a financial crisis will inevitably arise in the life of every business enterprise. Capacity to take a punch and bounce back could depend on the adequacy and availability of back up funds. In absence of a cash reserve, a company and its principal owners could end up out of business. In many cases, business failures can be traced to sudden adverse economic or financial mishaps.

For most small companies working capital is synonymous with emergency capital. Your rainy day stash not only serves to cover cost of operations for a reasonable period but also serves as a fail-safe for both personal and business emergencies.

In terms of defining a safe level of savings, personal financial planners commonly recommend maintaining at least three months costs of living. Intuitively this seems reasonable based possible disruptions in employment and lead time for securing another job. By comparison business enterprises face far more uncertainty. Their minimum emergency savings arguably should be more than three months cost of operations.

Often for business owners both critical personal and company related factors are intertwined. For instance, the non-renewal of a commercial line of credit, bankruptcy of a major customer, change of laws, loss of a key employee or a business downturn not only has the potential to deplete business earnings, but also devastate a business owner's source of personal income. A typical business owner has multiple family livelihoods to worry about as well.

With so many variables to consider even a savings or investment reserve aimed at two months operating expenses may not be sufficient savings for emergency or backup purposes for the owner of a business. More likely, the minimum dollar threshold should be business specific and tied to available financing sources including lines of credit as well as other forms of liquid assets.

For entrepreneurs launching a start-up, the threshold for a cash reserve may need to be greater relatively speaking. During ramp up of a new venture, sales forecasts and expense budgets may vary significantly from the forecast. Likewise, cash collections from customer sales may lag much longer than expected. Generally, revenue and expense patterns tend to be highly volatile. In addition, operators usually confront a steep learning curve especially if they have no prior business experience.

On the other, even an established business may be vulnerable to the whims of a wide range of troublesome economic forces. For example, credit may tighten in the overall economy. In periods of tight credit and fear of business downturn banks and other financial institutions are less inclined to renew or extend credit even to some long standing customers. Because banks usually reserve the right to review a credit line periodically and decide whether to cancel, it always makes sense to have a back up fund. Recent history indicates sole reliance on bank credit as a lifeline can be a mistake.

In general, business owners should err on the side of maintaining backup funds in excess of their calculated minimums. Even with a well-conceived back-up plan, actual experience may vary drastically from forecast.

It is always better to prepare for the worst case scenario since the best case will always take care of itself.

Business Worth

Unlike residential real estate there are no well-publicized listings to track the market values of privately owned businesses on a daily basis. Even if you find a source of information it probably would not be indicative of the true market price of a private company because so many subjective as well as objective factors come into play.

For most privately owned companies a significant amount of the owners' personal wealth is tied up in the business. It behooves anyone in this position to take every feasible measure to boost the market value of their investment over time in hopes that an eventual sale will yield a handsome capital gain.

A complete discussion of the many technical and judgmental approaches to business valuation is beyond the focus of this book. Nevertheless, it is feasible to offer a brief discussion of the rudiments of business valuation concepts and principles.

Ordinarily, parties to the sale of a business attempt to assess tangible and intangible qualities. While certain assets may be valued as a group, others are separated and appraised on an individual basis. On the other hand, buyers are sometimes only interested in purchasing certain assets rather than the purchasing a company as a whole.

The projected future income of a business usually sets the bar as the dominant pricing consideration. Potential future income provides the basis for what amounts to a price conversion process. Usually, the buyer will determine a value, discounted by a certain interest rate, based on projected cash flows to be received in future years. When the future cash flows are relatively reliable this present value method of valuation is generally considered the best guideline.

Potential future income provides the basis for what amounts to a price conversion process.

On the contrary, in certain industries a multiple of gross sales over several recent years is used as the standard rule of thumb in valuing a business. In these situations, business values are weighted more on top line revenues rather than bottom-line net cash flows. Other adjustments for assets and assumption of liabilities may also be taken into account in arriving at the overall valuation of a business.

In light of a multitude of business valuation technique and methodology, it pays to consult with CPAs, Attorneys and brokers familiar with industry practice. It is also important to consciously and systematically manage the value of your business like any other investment in your personal portfolio. It pays to assess your portfolio often and realign resources as deemed appropriate.

Many times, the value of a business is influenced by intangible considerations. One major intangible that reflects reputation, image, and brand is goodwill. Goodwill may also be tied up in customer contracts, operating systems, technical training and expertise. While these items typically do not get reported on the balance sheet or income statement they could be a critical element for business valuation and sale purposes.

Companies that possess precious intellectual property by way of customized software, patents, copyrights and licenses may also be valued based on projected worth of these items. In terms of appraisal legal protected rights may be highly valued. Of course, proof of legal title and ownership is crucial. In the end, you must be able to validate your rights and legal authority to make an asset transfer.

Likewise, your staff along with their employment contracts could be of high value in a service enterprise where specialized labor is key. With an ample legal framework the buyer may have less fearful of a mass exodus after the business is exchanged.

In some cases, a record of repairs and maintenance on major office and operating equipment will serve to boost value. Also, possessing legal authority to transfer manufacturer warranties and other protections could carry notable worth. The more you are able to measure the worth of every asset in your business portfolio, the more effective you stand to be in planning to ensure that every significant business asset will continue to hold its value.

Finally, the quality of your financial statements and tax returns will invariably carry added significance. Buyers usually place a great deal of reliance on them to support their suppositions regarding a business. To the extent they lack consistency or reliability this will tend to bring down business value.

It is safe to assume some of the variables discussed will be pivotal to the sales price of virtually every business. The future sales price of a business could be impacted negatively or positively based on current decisions of management. To maximize future value it is wise to study established practices of business valuation for your industry.

Pathways to Exit

Seasoned business veterans agree, in order to launch a successful business you need an overarching business strategy covering entry, operations and exit. Unfortunately, far too often the exit plan is put on the backburner or completely ignored until the business owner gets in a pinch.

Exit planning is critical in case sale or transfer of a privately owned company is necessitated by illness, disability or premature death. Under these circumstances a well-formulated exit strategy is crucial. With most private business owners transferring their ownership by succession or outright sale, it is important to be familiar with different business exit options and strategies.

In many family owned and operated businesses, transfer by succession is the goal. Ideally, transfer by succession requires careful advance planning and preparation. Grooming a family member or an insider to take over the business is far from an easy proposition. The person or persons under consideration for succession will probably need time to be properly trained and nurtured at the leadership level of the company. In addition, specialized management and industry training may be necessary. A succession plan predicated on succession is normally sequenced and coordinated to build talent and capabilities of the chosen successor. Otherwise, the person may be unprepared and jeopardize the health of the business.

Even when the succession process is tightly managed and guarded, there is no certainty the plan will come to fruition. The heir apparent may leave the employ of the company or simply later decline the invitation to take on ownership. On the other hand, as principal owner you could have a change of heart about their suitability for business ownership. Any of these developments could throw a succession plan off track. Therefore, a strategy for outright business sale should never be summarily discarded.

An exit strategy based on selling a business also requires strategic preparation and planning. First, the plan should be both flexible and adaptable. For example, a business owner might consider selling ownership to others in increments by doling out a portion of stock to them over a specific time interval, say every five years if they continue to work for the business. Public companies are widely known to use a version of this approach with a grant of restricted employee stock options. The approach grants stock benefits but also creates an incentive for the best people to stay. Ideally, this also gives high level management personal stake in the outcome of business performance.

A simple plan to exit by selling the business in the future will necessitate identifying potential types of buyers far in advance. You also should gauge marketability, pricing metrics and other factors that could influence sale prospects. Advance preparation should also allow for a business marketing strategy to be devised. Business brokers are readily available to offer assistance.

On the other hand, with the support of an investment banker a business owner may consider taking their company "public," by offering ownership interest to the general public. This strategy is another way to cash out by converting private business interests to public ownership. This path will require extensive consideration of cost, complexity and potential gain. Only a small fraction of businesses meet the extensive criteria to become a "public company."

Many aspects of developing an exit strategy are simply a matter of commonsense. Think for a moment about the steps most people take to avoid losing money on a home purchase. When choosing residential property most will evaluate their family needs and lifestyle. However, perhaps more important is how salable the property will be in the future. In essence, most people evaluate resale proposition even before they buy.

Homebuyers and entrepreneurs share the same economic objective as it relates to resale. In the case of entrepreneurs, they too have to assess the prospects of resale and make prudent upgrades to help their business value to appreciate. Just like homeowners business executives have to take care to make improvements and renovations to their property.

When it comes to enhancing a business investment, entrepreneurs should operate with the mentality that regular service and maintenance is incumbent. Moreover, it is essential to wisely invest in operations, infrastructure, systems and personnel development in order to stand to reap maximum gain in the future. In fact, exit preparation and planning should begin on day one.

Brain Storming

Even the most enlightened entrepreneur has less chance to succeed in the absence of competent highly qualified personal guidance from others outside of the company. Inevitably people on the inside have a tendency to become wedded to the boss, lose independence and objectivity when it comes to critical strategies and choices.

One way for companies to guard against becoming stagnant in mindset is to bring in outside business advisors to help plan business strategy, tactics and goals. These groups of people are sometimes informally referred to as a "kitchen cabinet." The more formal description is Board of Advisors. The members often consist of a combination of mentors, family and friends as well as professional lawyers, accounts and others.

Why establish a brain trust? With so many complex and strategic decisions on the table to make, people in business can least afford to lose focus, overlook opportunity or simply grow fatigued. With the constant pressure of critical decision making, the need for a reliable support base is critical.

Most large public companies establish a more formal think tank known as a Board of Directors. This group typically has ultimate responsibility for governance of the affairs of the company. The Board is charged with management oversight and helping to navigate uncharted waters. Such boards are typically compromised of people with rich business experience and insight. In addition to an oversight role, Boards of Directors can be extremely valuable for strategic planning purposes as well.

It is not complicated to formally establish a Board. The two most common models are relatively straight forward. They are known as a Board of Directors or board of advisors. A formal Board of Directors normally has to be legally approved by the corporation's shareholders or members of the limited liability company. The decisions and resolutions of a Board of Directors are legally binding on management. By contrast, recommendations and advice offered by a Board of Advisors generally are nonbinding.

Many investors and lenders consider a board to be a very important component of the management infrastructure. In fact, highlighting the educational and business backgrounds of board members in a business plan generally adds value to the plan. Those who have served in the past on the boards of successful companies will certainly cast a favorable image of your business. Just like for large public companies, an outside leadership group can help map strategy to circumvent a bad outcome for privately owned businesses also.

Many investors and lenders consider a board to be a very important component of the management infrastructure.

In addition providing guidance to executive management, members of the board are often a handy source of leads for new customers and investors. People intricately acquainted with the business model and operations also can be effective advocates for entrepreneurs in the early stages of development.

Boards are also a viable avenue for gaining access to specialized talent and expertise; such as, engineering, architecture, computer science and other specialized fields. Likewise, persons with extensive business experience may be willing to support the business through participation on a board. Oddly, it might be desirable to have someone on your board who previously failed in business. Their knowledge and experience could be invaluable essentially for the lessons learned.

Another highly instrumental part of a company's support base is its team of professional advisors—lawyers, accountants, insurance advisors, real estate brokers, financial planners, etc. It is best in most cases to solicit their input and assistance prior to undertaking any major business decision. In fact, this approach is far less costly than seeking their advice for correcting mistakes on the back end.

Without the benefit of a kitchen cabinet or a Board of Directors, CEOs and managers tend to become wedded to one school of thought, thereby losing the advantage of another perspective. Regardless of size, no business can afford to be myopic in its approach in the marketplace. Accordingly, large and small businesses alike need a kitchen cabinet or Board to assure progress and competitiveness. Should your thinking falter or stray off track, the cabinet or Board will be in the perfect position to redirect the thought process.

Disaster Readiness

In recent times, disaster preparation has become a high priority for a growing number of companies. Virtually every business regardless of size stands to be devastated by a natural or human engineered disaster. In order to recover financially, adequate contingent preparations are essential. At a minimum, every company should develop a set of disaster plans. In so doing, the list of questions below could help to direct the focus:

- What type of catastrophic events are you most vulnerable to operationally, managerially and administratively?
- How probable are these unfortunate events likely to occur?
- In the worst case, what would be the financial, legal and operational costs?
- Are company personnel set to manage a recovery process or will this require outside contractors and/or be dependent on public emergency assistance?
- If the company officer, contractor or outside party with primary responsibility for crisis management is unavailable, who else will be tapped to act as a surrogate to direct emergency response?

Your company's level of disaster readiness could determine whether it survives or falters after a tragedy. Commonly referred to as "Acts of God" in contracts, events such as tornado, hurricane, or severe weather storm could be crippling. There are also man-made incidents of crisis that can have a terrible impact. Needless to say, most of these risks cannot be eliminated. However, prudent measures can be taken to relieve the extent of damage.

Fortunately, in most jurisdictions local, State and Federal authorities have paved the way with documented programs and best practices for emergency response. Public resource guides covering channels of information dissemination and emergency response protocols are now widely available. For most companies this means they only need to craft limited contingency plans that feed into public resources.

On an individual basis emergency plans and preparations may vary based on company size, geographic location, technological resources and many other factors. Nevertheless, disaster plans will normally share some common fundamental elements as listed:

Disaster Planning Components

EMPLOYEE INFORMATION

Contact Information
Phone Tree
Transportation Alternatives
Emergency Housing Options
Financial Needs
Childcare Availability
Disaster Pay and Overtime Policies

KEY CONTACTS

Customers
Banks
Partners and Investors
Insurance Agents
Accountants
Lawyers

UTILITIES

Police, Fire and Rescue
Suppliers and Vendors
Contact Information
Geographic Diversity
Back-Up Sources
Credit Arrangements

PREPARATORY MEASURES

Written Policies
Operations Manual
Training
Simulations

Disaster Planning Components

BUSINESS FUNCTIONS

- Most Critical
- Allowable Downtime
- Legal Obligations to Customers, Creditors
- Recovery Locations
- Internal Communications Plans
- External Communications Plans
- Computer Networks and Back-Up
- Software Programs
- Inventory
- Equipment
- Vehicles
- Utilities
- Payroll
- Regulatory Requirements
- Accounts Payable
- Accounts Receivable

Naturally, to ensure that an emergency response plan is fully operational periodic tests similar to a routine fire drill should be planned. Each year some organizations use crisis specific conditions for this purpose in what are called "table top" exercises. Every three years they may engage in a full blown emergency response practice. This work is essential to maintain readiness. In today's world, emergency preparation is absolutely indispensable.

NOTABLE REFLECTIONS AT A GLANCE

- The essential forms of the life support for business owners include health, disability, life and long-term care.
- The standard level of cash back-up for emergencies is higher for entrepreneurs.
- Maximizing business value requires maintaining and growing the worth of significant business assets.
- Exit strategies and planning should begin prior to opening operations.
- Boards of Advisors and Directors serve to strengthen strategic planning and preparation.
- Disaster planning is critical to minimize the risk of devastation.

CHAPTER TWELVE

Pinpoint Strategic Priorities... Stockpile Reserves

| *The Journey* |

Losing money is not BJ's biggest fear. Instead, he is most fearful the company will not be positioned to secure financial backing for growth. He envisions competing in the global marketplace in the not too distant future, but realizes it will be very difficult to finance expansion through conventional bank financing. Instead, from the very start BJ would like to put aside a percentage of profits earned and use this as seed money to explore new markets, enlarge capacity and develop new products.

On the other hand, Taylor's main goal is current income. She believes aggressive growth will not allow for ample amount of distributions to the owners. In fact, she wants to form an agreement on specific guidelines for when and how much profit will be made available for distribution to owners on an annual basis. She also wants the partners to agree on their regular compensation levels.

Finally, prior to setting a launch date for the joint venture, BJ recommends engaging a tax professional to evaluate thebasic income tax ramifications of their plans. Although the partners expect the business will incur operating losses for the first two years, they believe it will generate substantial profits thereafter.

Lack of reserves is often the cause of business failure. Indeed this flaw can be found in otherwise promising business plans. If there is no strategy for stockpiling fund reserves, most companies will be at higher risk to implode in case of emergency. Far too often, entrepreneurs stop the strategic process short for this critical juncture. The more funding can be internally produced the less dependence a business will have on funds from outside sources in dire circumstances.

Some companies also fail to identify strategic planning pinpointing their strategic priorities. If you don't have financial priorities, your business may find itself always drifting aimlessly, buried in debt, constantly in a state of flux financially.

The focus of this chapter is on long-term strategic planning and budgeting for purposes of building fund reserves.

CHAPTER HIGHLIGHTS:

- Sustaining Reserves
- Tax Planning Templates
- Disciplined Saving Strategies
- Business Investment
- Rewarding Investors
- Debt Reduction

Tax Reserve

Virtually every profitable business faces the constant challenge of minimizing their income tax expense through effective tax planning. Income tax planning is essential not only to minimize expense but to avoid delinquent payments that could result in penalties, liens or seizures of business assets.

For businesses and self-employed individuals prosperous enough to have tax worries, income tax expenses should be estimated in advance and budgeted. Unlike expenses incurred in the ordinary course of business the government will not compute your income tax expense nor invoice on a monthly basis. As a business, it's your job to make these calculations annually based on your projected bottom line.

In a progressive tax rate system a higher tax rate percentage is applied as your income rises. Therefore, a flat line estimate of tax expense usually will not suffice. Likewise, intuitive judgments most always prove to be unreliable. Nevertheless, a gross miscalculation could not only mean underestimating real costs but, a situation where your company does not have enough cash to satisfy Uncle Sam.

As a safeguard against underfunding, businesses and self-employed individuals should estimate and make tax payments on a quarterly basis. In fact, those who fail to make quarterly estimated tax payments may be subject to penalties. Essentially, the rule imposes a savings discipline designed to help keep businesses from falling dangerously behind in paying income taxes.

On the positive side quarterly estimated tax deposits serve to reduce financial exposure for any unpaid income taxes at the end of the tax year. Without such a cushion, many businesses could experience a profitable year but find themselves struggling to pay off the year's income tax expense.

In addition to budgeting for quarterly estimated tax payments, small business owners and investors have to determine for tax purposes how best to structure their own compensation. For many small and closely held business owners this is a choice between taking W-2 wages versus being responsible for an allocation of taxable business earnings. Deciding on an optimal division is complicated because there is no hard and fast rule for determining what constitutes an employee-shareholder's "reasonable compensation" according to tax regulation. This is a pivotal concern when shareholders are also carried as employees on the books.

If not carefully planned and properly classified, income attributed to business earnings could be a double whammy in terms of taxation to company employee-owners. With potential for taxes at the owner and worker level, shareholders quickly discover that income tax planning is not for the faint at heart.

In estimating the bottom line for income tax purposes adjustments will have to be made due to restrictions on the timing. Certain deductions are allowable depending on the type of expense deduction, tax rules vary considerably. The critical factor may be on the timing of an expenditure (that is, whether funds were spent during a specific tax year), income level (that is, eligibility for deductions may phase out at certain income thresholds) or the type of legal entity (corporation, limited liability company, or sole proprietorship).

As suggested because of the litany of tax rules and regulations it may be difficult to reliably estimate annual income tax expense. Nevertheless, entrepreneurs have no choice but to make a good faith attempt to come as close as possible to the ultimate actual tax amount.

Tax deductions are typically contingent on timing (funds being spent in a specific time period), income level (benefits may be restricted or phased out with income) or type of legal entity (corporation, limited liability company, or sole proprietorship).

Tax planning considerations also differ depending on the type of legal entity involved. In some areas sole proprietorships, limited liability companies and corporations are treated differently for tax purposes. With these variations in mind and in order to minimize their tax expense overall, many small business owners favor a legal entity type that will combine the reporting of their business and personal income for income tax purposes. These so called "pass through" exceptions may help to avoid double taxation and to some degree streamline tax reporting.

A bare bones chart that provides a basic conceptual framework of the interlocking effects of the legal and tax structure of legal business entities is illustrated below:

SOLE PROPRIETORSHIP

1. *Taxable Income*—Income tax plus subject to self-employment tax (the equivalent of employee and employer's payroll taxes).
2. *Distributions to Owner*– Non-taxable (previously reported taxable income).

LIMITED LIABILITY COMPANY/PARTNERSHIP

1. *Taxable Income*—Taxable to members at their applicable individual marginal tax rates and subject to self-employment tax.
2. *Distribution to Members*—Non-taxable (previously reported as taxable income).
3. Guaranteed Payments to Members (for services rendered) — Taxable to recipient at individual marginal rates.

CORPORATION

1. *Taxable Income*—Taxable at corporation's applicable marginal income tax rates.
2. *Distributions to Shareholders (dividend)*—Taxable to individual shareholder at individual rates.
3. *Wages (for services rendered)*—Taxable to receipt shareholder at individual marginal tax rates.

SUBCHAPTER S CORPORATION

1. *Taxable Income*—Taxable to individual shareholder at applicable individual marginal tax rates.
2. *Distribution to Shareholders*—Non-taxable (previously taxed).
3. *Wages*—Taxable to individual at applicable individual marginal tax rate.

As the flow chart suggests there are many facets of income tax law that have the potential to cause a financial plan to go askew. Given the breath of twists and turns a savvy CEO is wise to seek professional guidance.

For most entrepreneurs and leaders it would be misuse of their time to attempt to stay abreast to the nuances and technicalities associated with changing tax laws. Without enlisting the advice and counsel of a qualified tax professional they might slide in a deep hole and become caught in an endless game of tax catch up.

Generation Skipping

Once a company has set aside adequate provisions to pay its income taxes, the CEO should give strong consideration to budgeting funding to develop the next generation of profitable business lines and enterprises. Suffice it to say, mobilizing a start-up operation, a new venture or new product line will usually involve some up front funding above and beyond the operating budget. In the absence of a designated fund earmarked for financial support the most promising ideas and opportunities might otherwise get put and left on the back shelf.

Ideally, funds budgeted for developing the next generation of business lines should be derived internally rather than financed from the outside. In order for this to be feasible, dollars may have to be specifically budgeted as a set aside in the cash flow plan. Once a specific venture has been formed any future costs should be treated as an ordinary business expense.

There are no hard and fast rules on how much or in what manner to establish a reserve fund for next generation strategies. However, it stands to reason most companies start with a simple estimate of labor time, expert consulting, travel and administrative costs.

A shining example of a company that invests handsomely in working to develop the next generation of technology products and services is Microsoft. Microsoft regards these investments as a strategic imperative. The company's stance was probably best described in a Wall Street Journal article entitled, "Behind Microsoft's Bid to Gain Cutting Edge."

> *When Bill Gates announced his plan to retire, Craig Mundie was appointed the company's chief research and strategy thinker.*
>
> *As reported in the Wall Street Journal, "The challenge, he says, is anticipating what new technologies have the potential to be- come a big business for the company, or conversely, to threaten its foundation."*
>
> *Microsoft maintains research facilities all over the globe, and Mr. Mundie travels an estimated 200,000 miles per year meeting with researchers and customers. He identifies potentially viable technologies, and coordinates development of compatible products in various parts of the world.*
>
> *The firm invests in immature technologies considered promising and helps develop them into commercially viable products. The company also purchases potentially competitive and innovative firms to acquire their technologies. Finally, Microsoft often uses small groups of experts from a variety of functions to develop and test specialized products.*
>
> *As Mr. Mundie described it, "You've got to have a small number of people who think that it's their job to take risks ... I view my job, in part, as making sure that the company supports the things that take time but end up being big."*[1]

Even with a philosophical commitment to remain proactive, according to some analysts Microsoft could face a very rocky road ahead. As we enter a new millennium of technology they wonder whether Microsoft, among other technology giants, will preserve by keeping pace with more nimble companies that press to hard to lead the way in introducing new innovations.

> *Analysts have argued that its (Microsoft) fade was part of the natural progression for all companies. The life cycle of innovation, adoption, missteps and irrelevancy is the inevitable fate of all companies. It suffered the "innovator's dilemma" of overemphasizing its current business lines. This led to a failure to develop new technologies and profitable businesses. In the end, the thinking goes, it was a victim of its own success.*

Although the depth of Microsoft's challenges may be considerably more complex than the average entrepreneurial company, the competitive forces it must confront to remain vibrant and profitable are essentially the same for any business. Notwithstanding Microsoft's incredible record of growth and financial success, no company can afford to rest on their laurels.

The global economy will be impacted by population growth in developing countries such as China, India and Indonesia.

In light of changing world demographics it behooves every business to continually look out on the horizon and ask, what business opportunities have we cultivated for the future? Keep in mind the world's population is estimated to increase by approximately 2 billion people to 8 billion by 2020. According to the National Research Council of Canada (NCRC), the bulk of the growth will occur in developing countries such as China, India and Indonesia. Increased globalization should impact the rate of population expansion throughout the world. "Asian culture will profoundly shape global interactions, societal values and behaviors."[2]

The Wall Street Journal reported:

> *Charles Reinhard, director of portfolio strategy at asset-management firm Neuberger Berman, estimates that companies in the S&P 500 derive about 30% of their revenue from abroad, up from 22% five years ago. U.S. companies also get a big chuck of profits from overseas operations: According to data from the Commerce Department, foreign subsidiaries accounted for about 24% of U.S. after tax corporate profits in 2006, com- pared with 17% a decade ago. (The number does not include exports from the U.S.)*[3]

As the global marketplace evolves many believe entrepreneurial businesses will be in position stand to benefit the most assuming they have a strategic plan. Internet technology provides a convenient step ladder for small agile companies to mount a formidable marketing campaign to serve a world market.

Major Replacements

Reinvesting dollars back into a company in order to keep it running smoothly is analogous to paying for regular automobile service and maintenance. In order to reasonably insure that your vehicle will hold up over time and continue to operate like new, most people concede the need to reinvest in maintenance and up keep. Likewise, on a routine basis companies should plan to reinvest in their operational platform to keep it up to speed.

Defining how much and when to accumulate resources for major replacements should be a CEO and executive management responsibility. In discharging the duty management should start by reviewing and analyzing core operations with the intent to identify and discern major replacement items that should be pre-funded. For instance, it may be critical for companies that owns and manages real estate to establish a reserve for high cost capital replacements with the goal of gradually stockpiling a special reserve fund.

Over the long term, footing the costs of roof replacements, re-paving roadways as well as rebuilding heating and ventilation systems are inevitable and indispensable. Planning and scheduling ahead of time to replace structural items can afford the opportunity to either save in advance or search out the most economical financing arrangement.

To no surprise, service enterprises also are not immune from the need to reinvest in infrastructure. They too should be concerned with updating or replacing central technology; communication devices, transportation equipment, training aids and other items essential to ongoing operations. From a funding perspective, it would be unwise to delay the accumulation of resources and instead depend on the future availability of outside funding. The best way to level off the cost of major replacements in the future is through a monthly set aside.

Unlike capital intensive businesses, service enterprises tend to be less inclined to prepare themselves with regard to pre-fund infrastructure replacements. Knowingly or unknowingly the vast numbers of service businesses live in the here and now without a sense of urgency. On the flipside the nonchalance could contribute to a higher rate of business failure.

Strategic funding needs and requirement will undoubtedly vary from one business to the next. Savvy leaders resist the urge to procrastinate. They choose to be proactive by landing a special fund.

Critical analysis of financial requirements in terms of hard costs as well as inflation, business growth and other relevant economic factors is important. Likewise, key financial indicators such as the consumer price index, interest rate trends and credit availability should not be ignored.

The overriding objective of a fund for business reinvestment is simply to create a savings sufficient to underwrite all or at least a significant portion of any major infrastructure replacements.

Long range business plansmust be defined to ascertain the funding needs and requirements of a replacement reserve.

Contingency Fund

A common mistake capable of quickly derailing a financially sound business is failure to establish a contingency reserve fund. This type of resource provision recognizes the need to set aside funding for events outside of management's control that could a costly adverse outcome.

Where a strong risk exists for a significant outlay of funds due to a future event, a contingency reserve should be considered. The types of events could range from escalations in insurance premiums, product liability, warranties as well as adverse judgments in lawsuits.

Absorbing a major financial hit at a time when a company's operating cash is at its lowest level could be disastrous. In fact, in some instances the mere survival of a business could be threatened. That said, the need for a contingency reserve fund is self-evident.

On the other hand, determining how much to safely set aside may come down to conservative forecasts. To make a reasonably safe estimate of financial exposure may require consultation with a business lawyer, CPA or other qualified professional.

Even contingencies of a less magnitude than a major lawsuit should be reviewed and evaluated periodically. For example, equipment acquired under lease may provide for a buy-out option at the end of the lease term at a relatively significant cost. Conceivably, a business loan may entail a balloon payment, a shareholder's agreement, an investor buyout clause, a landlord's lease or business relocation obligation.

The overriding concern is that unfunded and unanticipated major expense will surface at a time when operating cash is at its lowest level.

In terms of ordinary operations it also may be wise to budget savings for premium deductions on commercial liability and casualty insurance. Indeed, some organizations actually save money by accumulating funds to provide for self-insurance in whole or in part.

Even on a foundational level it may not be easy to reliably estimate the appropriate amount of reserve funding. For example, liability associated with extended product and service warranties may be difficult to estimate. The number of future warranty and service claims may be indeterminable especially for a relatively new product line. Just the same in order to minimize financial exposure, it is wise to budget savings based on a good faith estimate.

Businesses should treat potential loss of a major contract as another form of financial contingency. General and government contracting businesses routinely budget with the potential for lags between major contracts. In this industry a gap between beginning new contracts after completion of existing ones is not uncommon. Without a set aside to pay for ongoing expenses, contractors could be forced to downsize, cut their regular labor force or possibly sell off operating assets. Many seasonal businesses operate with the same type of risks in mind. They too could experience a substantial fall off in revenue due to extreme weather conditions.

The first step toward building a reserve is to devise a list of the type of major unexpected costs that could arise.

Lastly, a periodic review of various legal agreements could reveal the potential for future financial obligations worth budgeting. For example, legal documents that contain penalty or forfeiture clauses for late payment, late delivery, or incomplete performance. Depending on current business conditions it may be more or less likely that these clauses will be invoked. From a contingency reserve perspective the possibility should be considered.

In essence, the driving force behind saving funds for contingencies is simply to avoid the risk of financial collapse as a result of adverse outcomes.

Cash Rewards

At a minimum virtually every savvy investor expects to be rewarded financially especially in good times. Financial return is compensation for the risk assumed in making an uninsured investment.

Typically investors look to be rewarded in two ways namely, through the receipt of cash payments or dividends and by appreciation in the market value of their investment. Unfortunately, stock values of private businesses are not reported on national stock exchanges. Therefore, any true increase in the market value of shares held in a privately owned business is not readily determinable. With this component of financial return off the radar, cash payouts or dividends take on far more added importance.

Even when earnings and profits are reported in the financial statements this does not necessarily mean expendable funds are readily available to pay dividends. In fact, very rarely will the retained earnings reported in the balance sheet fully reveal a company's capacity to payout dividends.

For most companies the lion's share of retained earnings (often labeled members' capital for a limited liability company or owners' equity for a sole proprietorship) is tied up in accounts receivables and operating assets such as machinery equipment and buildings. Therefore, when evaluating the potential or capacity to make cash distributions owners are wise to look beyond reported retained earnings. The decision also should not be made in vacuum simply based on cash deposit at banks. Rarely can a company afford to risk draining cash needed for working capital even as retained earnings is rising.

In determining when and how much you can afford to reward investors, the first place to begin is with an examination of your company's overall level of liquidity. Liquidity or free cash not only should be assessed in light of short-term strategic priorities but minimum working capital needs.

CEOs are often conflicted and tormented by a desire to handsomely reward investors while keeping the business positioned to continue to fund on-going operations. These two objectives are sometimes difficult to mesh.

In public companies, Board of Directors are empowered not only to help decide dividend policy, but also to make the final call. They too become conflicted at times. Their dilemma is to balance investor and Wall Street expectations with operating cash needs and requirements.

Retained earnings reported in the balance Sheet may not represent cash in liquid form.

In entrepreneurial businesses timing, manner and approach for rewarding investors should be carefully managed. Sound business planning and judgment is paramount. As a boost of wisdom, private companies may elect to form an advisory or board of directors. This group of people can serve as a brain trust regarding a variety of significant decisions.

In order to map out coherent dividend strategies a CEO might also enlist the services of a tax advisor to avert unintended consequences. Keep in mind, payout dividends for a corporation is facilitated with after tax dollars. Professional guidance may be needed because normally this will subject the recipient shareholders to so called, double taxation. Double taxation arises when income tax is paid once by a corporation and then again by its shareholders. On the other hand, there are ways for a qualifying small business to avoid this dilemma.

Fortunately, the law provides that relatively small private corporations may opt out of a structure that might otherwise result in double taxation. However, there are a rigid set of standards to qualify as a Subchapter S for income tax purposes including maximum allowable number of investors, requirement that all investors must be individuals and U.S. citizens.

In public companies a powerful board of directors determines if, when and how much dividends to pay out.

An important potential key advantage is a Subchapter S corporation just like LLCs, partnerships and sole proprietorships serves as a "pass through entity." Therefore, rather than the business itself paying income taxes, the burden for reporting and paying income tax one time only falls on the individual shareholders.

Suffice it to say there can be many downsides to a Subchapter S election as well. Tax elections are not void of traps and possible negative unintended consequences. This is the primary reason for business owners to seek professional advice and counsel prior to executing major decisions bearing potential tax consequences.

Debt Reduction

To avoid becoming too highly leveraged and thereby unable to pay debts as agreed, businesses will sometimes opt to either work toward reducing debt or to convert loans to equity. Even when ample cash is available to service debt there could be certain operating advantages to reducing the level of debt.

We start with this basic proposition, too much debt puts extreme pressure on profits and cash flow. It also hinders a company's flexibility to actively pursue new businesses and product lines.

Eligibility for refinancing in the future should never be taken for granted.

Depending on cash position deleveraging or reducing debt may be a very effective business strategy. Many companies take this path especially when their cash balance is heavy or while experiencing a robust business cycle. As earlier suggested public companies often negotiate convertible debt, that is, debt that can be converted to equity in the form of stock. A similar approach can be used in entrepreneurial businesses. In these cases, the move may be to convert loans made to the company by principal owners and shareholders into more stock.

For all the good it provides at various times during a business' life cycle, most every company at some point aspires to reduce debt if for no more than create more breathing room financially. Implementing a basis plan could also entail identifying the most economical opportunities for refinancing loans at a lower interest rate. Debt capital is much like any other commodity; price and terms are key distinguishing qualities.

Refinancing could also be a function of more favorable terms. For example, terms associated with loan maturity, collateral, and limits on certain financial ratios may be of equal or greater importance than pricing. At the end of the day, developing a debt management strategy is vital to business success as product pricing and cash flow planning.

Brighter Horizons

To help relieve long term debt pressure, some companies elect to establish a debt sinking fund. With the understanding that commercial debt sometimes provides the only viable means for a company to gain access to capital to finance accounts receivable, inventory and equipment there may a time in the business life cycle where the level of future debt obligations becomes a haunting thought. It may be perceived as onerously burdensome on future profits and cash flow. That said, it may be preferable simply to work toward paying down long term future obligations.

Future long term obligations come in different varieties. For example, under a shareholder or member buy sale agreement. In the absence of adequate insurance coverage a company could be forced to sell off operating assets to meet the commit. Savings is a way to avoid this type of predicament.

Early retirement of debt could be motivated by other financial considerations. For example, a loan covenant may stipulate maximum compensation for key executives, earnings available for distribution to owners, sale of certain business assets or other matters that are usually within management's sole discretion. At some junction these and other type of restrictions make the financing relationship less than desirable.

Future obligations that may be of greatest concern in terms of savings are those which peak within five years. Some commercial loans contain balloon or major principal payments that are legally required after a specific number of years. These loans may be structured with "a five year term and twenty year amortization." In this situation, lower monthly payment during the five year term of the loan would be followed by a substantial payoff at the end of the fifth year.

Strategically, a debt sinking fund should serve as a methodical way to build savings to retire long term debt when there is no legal obligation to do so a company has the option to use the funds as designated or for any other more compelling purpose. With this in mind you should think of it as a vehicle to make for brighter horizons.

Notable reflections at a glance

- A reserve for estimated taxes minimizes the risk of becoming delinquent.
- For long term sustainability reserves should be set aside to explore new product and service lines.
- Business reinvestment is essential to maintain a solid business infrastructure.
- A reserve for debt reduction serves to reduce dependency and cost of debt financing.

CHAPTER THIRTEEN

Champion Profitable Growth... Finish in the Black

| *The Journey* |

BJ and Taylor agree to an official launch date for their joint venture and turn their attention to growth projections. They agreed to strive to grow the company at an annual rate of twenty percent over the next three years. They also hope to squeeze out a profit by the end of the second year.

Taylor will concentrate on sales and marketing, while BJ's role will be mainly operations management. The team also agrees to form a board of advisors. Additionally, a meeting with legal counsel will be set to address legal structure.

Assuming their sales and operating objectives are achieved, BJ and Taylor will be able to qualify for private equity funding within three years. By year seven the company should be financially positioned to either take the company public or sell outright.

Athletes learn the basics of any sport before tackling sophisticated moves and strategies. Drawing from the analogy of an athlete in training, the healthy development of a business lies with entrepreneurs who stand to benefit greatly from proven financial methods and strategies for achieving profitable growth.

Growth per se can be a two edge sword; it can propel a business to new and glorious heights financially or condemn it to ruin. The cliché that some businesses grow themselves out of business contains many grains of truth. If you do not learn to avoid pitfalls, growth can inflict business harm financially and operationally.

Profitable growth draws a clear distinction between good and bad growth. Simply put, good growth represents new business that contributes financially to the bottom line and offers an intangible benefit by way of goodwill, customer satisfaction, employee retention, and productivity.

Profitable growth is measured by a strong rate of new sales revenues matched by a robust climb in net income. In contrast, bad growth is counterproductive and takes a heavy toll on customer service, operating efficiency and financial stability. In the long term, the costs of bad growth far outweigh the benefits.

This chapter focuses on cultivating and managing healthy growth.

CHAPTER HIGHLIGHTS:

- Balancing Growth and Profit
- Parameters of Healthy Growth
- Embracing Best Practices
- Strategic Preparation and Execution
- Capacity Building

The Balancing Act

The most significant task confronting the CEO of virtually every business is maintaining profitable growth. A company that masters the art is bound for long-term success and financial prosperity.

I deferred discussion of profitable growth to the very end because without the benefit of a working knowledge of the pros and cons and the dos and don'ts of financial management it could have been too daunting. Now the time is just right.

Have you ever wondered why a company with sales in the millions of dollars continually reports staggering net losses, or why a small business faced with overwhelming demand for its services suddenly declares bankruptcy? Many times the reason is not lack of growth, but lack of profitable growth.

Gateway Computer, once the third largest distributor of personal computers in the United States, provides a good example of the tribulations companies can confront while working to cultivate profitable growth.

Gateway, originally the TIPC Network, was founded by Ted Waitt on a South Dakota farm. Legend has it Mr. Waitt borrowed $10,000 to start the business and secured the loan with his grandmother's certificate of deposit.

Initially the company sold personal computer parts directly to consumers via telephone. Within two years, the company was offering complete computer systems. Gateway's strategy was simple: offer knowledgeable buyers full-featured computer systems for approximately the same price as competitor's stripped down systems by eliminating resellers.

Gateway's approach was a success. Within ten years annual sales reached over $5 billion. Profitability began suffering shortly thereafter as the computer industry suffered from decreasing prices and over supply. During this period the company's sales increased 25% to 6.3 billion, but profitability decreased by 50% that year.

Mr. Waitt decided to make significant changes at Gateway. The firm's headquarters was moved to San Diego, primarily to make it easier to attract qualified personnel. Gateway entered into several strategic alliances with companies such as Sun Microsystems, Office Max and AOL to augment its capacity for new product development and product sales. The company expanded its lines of business to include consulting services. Finally, Gateway opened hundreds of Gateway Country Stores to sell computers at the retail level. The company planned to achieve sales revenues of $25 billion within five years.

These expansion strategies were considered risky and met with mixed success. The move out of Sioux City changed consumers' perceptions of Gateway and caused it to lose much of its down home image. Furthermore, experts estimated it cost $1.5 million to launch a Gateway Country store. Financing hundreds of stores put enormous financial stress on the company.

The retail expansion was not successful as the following three years proved. After several restructurings, Gateway closed all of its Country Stores. Gartner analyst Charles Smulders described the store closings:

> *It's a positive move for Gateway ... The stores were expensive to run, and margins are very thin in the consumer PC business ... Gateway held a 3.5 percent market share ... Gateway has been losing share for some time ... Gateway was unable to drive enough store traf-*

> *fic to justify the cost of operating the stores ... The margins they were able to make and the volumes they were able to drive just did not match the store investment.*

In the same year Gateway experienced a net loss of $114 million, or 35 cents per share, on revenues of $3.4 billion.

A year later Gateway acquired low-cost personal computer maker eMachines, which had annual sales of $1.1 billion and several years of profitable growth. The company was well-known for its product distribution through outlets such as Best Buy and Walmart.

Gateway's retail sales did increase as a result of this merger, and the company achieved market share of over 6% by 2006. While the company is profitable, margins keep getting squeezed. Gateway continues to look for ways to reduce operating costs and increase profitability.[1]

Gateway's struggles are indicative of the balancing act that surrounds growth management. At one time or another virtually every company will experience the pleasures and wrath of intense sales growth. A knowledge and understanding of the fundamentals of healthy growth will help smooth the tumultuous ride.

Sales Volume

How could a business otherwise survive without a steady flow of new sales and repeat business? Undoubtedly, growth is the primary driver for healthy business development. Intuitively, we know a certain level of annual growth in sales is needed simply to keep the doors open. However, to build real financial muscle every business has to achieve critical mass in sales revenue.

At critical mass, most businesses will be in a position to exercise significant buying and purchasing leverage. Size will translate into economic clout and open doors to greater cost savings and price discounts. However, critical mass is a relative concept. A smaller company may have a lower threshold than its larger counterparts.

In this sense, critical mass may require more sales volume than breakeven. For breakeven your profit margin must equal your operating, general and administrative expenses. After the threshold has been achieved, profit margins on any additional sales, flow directly to the positive bottom line.

On the other hand, think of critical mass as the magic point on the scale where a company can exercise influence and bargain more favorably with suppliers. More purchasing power alone may offer an economic advantage over less endowed peers. Similarly, price and purchasing advantages are usually extended to businesses with high growth potential. Suppliers offer price discounts to customers who purchase frequently and in increasing volumes, rather than companies that purchase sporadically or in small quantities.

Economic clout goes beyond discounts on merchandise purchases. For example, banks often offer special cost saving in the form of lower fees for loan origination, loan interest, checking and other bank services to commercial clients who utilize a package of banking services. Like many other suppliers of goods and services, financial institutions reward their more lucrative customer relationships.

In terms of resale value, the market price of a high sales volume company will usually be markedly higher than for a similar smaller company. This is especially true in industries that customarily base business values on multiples of annual gross sales revenues. In many cases, a strong volume has the effect of nullifying any significance that might otherwise be attached to a string of financial losses. Ideally, every business should aim for the total package: a handsome top line and profitable bottom line.

Growth Strategies

Devising an effective growth strategy does not mean planning to bring in any and all forms of new business. On the contrary, viable growth strategies focus on attracting and retaining "profitable customers." Generally speaking, quality of new business is just as important as quantity. A basic set of questions that may help to trigger a balanced focus on both quality and quantity are as follows:

How big are your ideal customers?

For commercial customers, consider characteristics such as annual revenues and number of employees. For retail customers, consider household income and household size.

Under what circumstances do clients need to purchase from you?

Selling to a company or individual who needs your product or service is far easier than selling to a potential client who does not see immediate value in your goods.

How often do they purchase and in what quantities?

All businesses love repeat buyers. Knowing who purchases most from you will help you plan your sales and marketing activities and determine when price discounts are advantageous.

Which potential clients can best afford your product or service?

You do not want to waste valuable sales and marketing resources pursuing companies only to find they cannot afford your goods. Similarly, few entrepreneurial businesses have the time or energy to chase slow paying clients.

As the list suggests, the clientele you target naturally dictates many other decisions ranging from promotional media and collateral material to business location and pricing. The more focused your target market is, the more effective your growth strategies are likely to be.

While a full discussion of particular marketing techniques would go far beyond the confines of this book, the more effective approaches usually reflect a combination of online promotions, direct advertising, word of mouth, customer referrals and, discount price incentives. Effective selling and marketing are no doubt keys to growing sales.

Growing a business organically usually requires a multidimensional marketing strategy. Digital platforms albeit through websites, social media and traditional media should be considered depending on the nature of the products and services involved.

Online crowdsourcing is an inexpensive way for new and existing businesses to test marketability and demand for new ideas, products and services. Crowdsourcing is a method of raising capital through the collective effort of friends, family, customers and individual investors. It can also stimulate contact with many prospective customers for purposes of soliciting their evaluation of product design, quality and pricing.

In essence, crowdfunding provides a way to tap into people's brains before undertaking a costly development and rollout plan. Essentially it has replaced focus groups which serve as the tool to gain qualitative market research. It is still advisable to utilize the expertise of a company that specializes in sifting through the ideas of crowds on behalf of online businesses. Crowdsourcing campaigns can also be facilitated with crowdsourcing software.

Another highly effective growth strategy for many small and large companies is expansion growth by acquisition. Acquisitions of other companies with an attractive customer base, distribution outlets or stellar reputation may be a viable growth technique. The approach can be applied in many different industries.

However, please be forewarned, acquiring another company requires careful investment analysis. Acquisition candidates must be evaluated in depth operationally, financially and legally. In other words, investing in another company to promote growth can also be a high risk proposition. First, the numbers have to make sense. When the acquirer lacks the necessary expertise to conduct a thorough analysis they usually engage a team of specialists for representation.

If any assessment proves positive, a combination of two separate businesses may enable the combined entity to eliminate duplicate expenses and absorb excess capacity. Likewise, the firms may realize economies of scale from blending technical expertise. For these reasons growth through acquisition should never be ruled out even by an entrepreneurial business. Hardly a day goes by when mergers and acquisitions are not reported in local and national business news.

While the average entrepreneurial business may not possess the investment capital of industry giants, growth by acquisition could be a plausible option with the right financing. Investment bankers aggressively pursue opportunities to package acquisition deals that offer major promise. The key question for them is whether the business combination will significantly enhance the earnings power of the companies involved and thereby, attract investor interest.

Healthy Business Expansion

Too much or too little growth will wreak havoc on the bottom line of any business. The secret to benefiting from growth lies in distinguishing healthy versus unhealthy growth. In other words you must have a strong sense of manageable limits. Moreover, when you exceed your company's financing or operating capacity, losses and instability may ensue.

A massive leap in sales growth can drain cash and drive up short term debt. This could endanger a company's ability to pay ordinary expenses on a timely basis. Similarly, a sudden jump in operating expenses could make it impossible for a growing company to service its debt.

The first test of feasibility is sufficiency of financing resources. Growing without adequate financing is likely to result in financial impairment. Without sufficient internal resources or "bridge financing," working capital will evaporate.

In addition, most companies face a functional restraint dictated by operating capacity. The simplest way to understand this limitation is to think in terms of maximum production capacity measured by the maximum capacity of equipment, physical plant and labor. Like a breakeven exercise you should ask the question for your business: "What levels of production can we comfortably handle?"

In a service enterprise, output capacity may not be easy to pinpoint. Metrics may have to be designed based on time studies or average completion of routine customer transactions. In essence, it is important to determine your staffs' daily, weekly or monthly limits recognizing over capacity may compromise customer service and quality.

Because conditions are subject to change, manageable growth limits and financing and operating capacities should be monitored and reevaluated periodically. Remember, exceeding reasonable bounds will tend to jeopardize the overall financial well-being of your company.

Boeing Co. learned first-hand that spiraling growth can have a crippling effect. Now, they conscientiously tempter growth and resist the temptation to overreach.

The Wall Street Journal reported on Boeings previous challenges:

> *At the turn of the century Boeing tried to ramp up production so quickly that suppliers were unable to make parts fast enough. Unfinished planes stacked up at its factories here, forcing managers to shut down production for a month to allow the strained supply chain to catch up. The colossal stumble led to a rare year-end loss and $2.6 billion in charges against earnings over two years.*
>
> *Building an aircraft requires a reported 367,000 parts from nearly 1,000 suppliers and can take years to complete. Boeing incurs much of the production cost before the customer pays off the $65 million price, and the delay in delivery of a plane or cancellation of an order by an*

airline can have devastating effects. Much can change during the time it takes to build a plane, and airlines have been known to cancel orders during recessions such as occurred after September 11, 2001.

Boeing management does not intend to make the same mistake twice. Although demand for new aircraft is increasing dramatically, the company intends to increase production gradually. According to Scott Carson, head of Boeing's Commercial Airplanes Unit, "Boeing will agree to a jump in production rates only if it can sustain the pace for at least a couple of years … We don't sell airplanes on the assumption that the factories have infinite ability to produce them."

Now Boeing uses a committee of senior managers from both the production and finance areas of the firm to approve major airline orders and associated delivery timetables. Available capacity at both Boeing and its suppliers is factored into the approval process.

Similarly, Boeing uses a team to manage airport delivery dates and backorders. As a result the company was able to deliver 398 airplanes, up 41% from deliveries three years prior. Management projected deliveries to increase to 445 and 520 respectively in the next two years.

Boeing's cautionary approach paid off financially. The Commercial Airplanes Unit's operating profit margins reached almost 10% up from the 6% achieved in the past. This self-restraint probably best exemplifies the wisdom of controlling growth.[2]

Boeing's lessons are indicative of the perils that uncontrolled growth creates. As a general rule a business should avoid unlimited growth and not set limits of growth strictly in response to demand. Service enterprises also can fall into the trap of becoming demand driven. In the final analysis, growth should never be allowed to outstrip the financing or operating capacity of a business.

Infrastructure Development

Preparing to grow profitably usually entails upgrading systems that support business services and operating production. A strong infrastructure is essential to withstand increased demand flow from added business activity. Otherwise, operating bottlenecks and disruptions are bound to occur.

These and other basic support systems facilitate adequate staffing, training, supplies and materials. Critical infrastructure also consists of budget controls, performance benchmarks and system of accounting. Without these prerequisites for managing growth, profitability is virtually impossible.

A strong reporting system is also a key to growth management systems that serve to prevent a false positive, that is, an erroneous conclusion that efficiency and productivity are at peak levels. Operating only based on what you intuitively think is a profitable platform is a recipe for disaster.

Throughout this book we have focused largely on key parts of business and financial infrastructure. Our study has extended from planning, tracking and monitoring performance to legal structure and risk controls. You do not want to experience a growth spurt without having your house in order.

In order to maintain profits as a business grows, accountability is crucial. Albeit the cost and use of resources by specific divisions, departments and projects illustrates the need for reliable information and feedback in real time and may make or break the bottom line. Entrepreneurs and CEOs cannot have an oversupply of convenient mechanisms for evaluating their business company-wide on a day-to-day and month-to-month basis.

Highly successful multinational companies like Toyota Motor Corporation are keenly aware of the hazards of rising inefficiency in the face of growth. As noted in a published article Toyota Motor Corporation relies on a close watch over performance, productivity and efficiency to remain on top:

> *Senior managers fear the company will suffer from the same arrogance which has derailed several other international car manufacturers. According to Ken Tomikawa, Toyota Canada president, "The enemy of Toyota is Toyota." Jeremy Cato of Merrill Lynch described Tomikawa's concern as follows:*
>
> *... he worries about the new, young, swaggering Toyota employees who have never experienced bad times and who seem to be comfortable with the idea that Toyota is just naturally superior to all the other auto makers.*
>
> *To avoid complacency, Toyota recently implemented significant improvements in its manufacturing processes and found ways to save substantial development and production costs.*[3]

Toyota's philosophy speaks to the need to continually revisit performance standards and incentives. If performance standards are not revisited, inefficiencies and complacency can undercut profits even in the face of strong sales growth.

Precautionary Measures

As the information in this chapter suggests, growth does not automatically translate to greater financial return. Many companies experience strong, consistent sales growth but show steadily declining profits. If a CEO does not spot trouble signs early, growth will only worsen earnings.

On the other hand, with sound planning and oversight, growth is the best avenue for maximizing financial returns. However, certain precautions must be taken. First, pricing and cost controls have to implemented. Additionally, cash from operations must be closely monitored and supplemented from time to time to maintain positive cash flow.

During a peak growth cycle you must be on guard for financial deterioration in the form of late payments to key vendors and build up accounts receivable. As growth peaks, maintaining stability will be a day-to-day challenge.

Financial percentages and ratios should be monitored frequently. Indicators that gauge working capital, accounts receivable turnover and cash flow coverage should be tracked closely and routinely.

Managing growth also requires making enhancements and upgrades to your business structure along the way and preferably in advance. Many companies with high growth potential falter, because these needs go unaddressed until the eleventh hour.

Preparing an updated business plan is also highly recommended. A variety of management needs and requirements will likely change in a significant way as your business grows. Your organizational blueprint should be complete with an organizational chart depicting any necessary changes in the division of duties and responsibilities. Organizational preparation also entails modifying written policies and procedures to better foster a productive work place.

Likewise, technology upgrades are essential. "IT strategy" is highly recommended. Similarly, personnel recruitment, training and development plan adjustments will be necessitated. Growth normally demands a more diverse set of job skills and staff composition.

Last but not least, growth management entails implementing financial safeguards known as internal controls. These controls represent a specific subset of financial controls aimed primarily at protecting assets from mishandling, theft or fraud and at assuring accuracy in financial accounting and reporting. Internal controls represent a highly functional system of checks and balances that focus on detecting financial errors and irregularities.

The Homestretch

For better or for worse and for richer or for poorer, entrepreneurs and CEOs have to take charge of the financial well-being of their companies. Many business veterans wish they had become intricately involved in the financial affairs from the get go.

As in any athletic endeavor, ultimately the head coach is responsible for getting the team ready to compete at a high level. He or she may delegate certain duties to assistants and team captains, but at the end of the day the head coach will be held accountable. It is a fine line between maximizing player talent and controlling team performance.

In an interview for Babson Insight, Herb Kelleher, CEO of Southwest Airlines discussed the methods it uses to promote the best performance.

"... we use scenario planning. We might ask 'what happens if a certain airline significantly contracts its fleet?' In response we pull together our ideas on how we might respond. You just can't predict what may happen and that's why I say: ready, aim, fire because opportunity won't be there unless you act quickly. It doesn't have to be perfect when you start it. This is what prevents many people from being quick, they want to be perfect. We'd rather go ahead imperfectly and improve as we go."[4]

The Road to MegaSuccess was aimed to help you redesign and improve your financial management game plan. Armed with knowledge, skill and proven strategies for success, I am confident you will indeed grow profitably. For ease of planning your moves in the future, the next and final chapter provides a graphic recap of the critical elements for enriching the bottom line.

NOTABLE REFLECTIONS AT A GLANCE

Profitable growth requires meticulous planning and oversight with the following guiding principles:

- Controlling growth means balancing financing and operating capacity.
- Profitable growth produces positive top and bottom lines.
- Sound management minimizes internal and external resources.
- Performance assessment must be a top priority.
- Successful businesses invest in growth and business development.

CHAPTER FOURTEEN

Practice the Mantra... Develop Muscle Memory

| *The Journey* |

The day following BJ and Taylor's final planning meeting BJ received a call from by a national business broker. To BJ's amazement the broker explained that the company is most Matrix's regarded as it's most formidable regional competitor was now up for sale. He encouraged BJ to seriously consider making a purchase offer.

The broker made a strong case for how the business acquisition could benefit Matrix financially. First, he stressed the seller's well established national customer base, compatibility of existing operating systems and a potential multiplier effect on Matrix's overall earnings. All things being equal, business combination could potentially catapult Matrix into the top ten percent of the entire industry.

On the other hand, already deeply immersed in the new deal with Taylor, BJ was conflicted about taking any additional investment risks. Nevertheless, he felt compelled at least to carefully evaluate the feasibility of the business acquisition. Accordingly, he decided once again to work through the same basic process of analysis he used in deciding whether to team up with Taylor.

The acquisition would double Matrix's sales volume, distribution network, and market share. The financial rewards would include much greater economies to scale in purchasing inventory, more efficient operating equipment, more convenient warehousing and other operational advantages. On the other hand, BJ also recognized the deal would require sophisticated forms of financing, involve major changes in management structure and call for upgrades in financial reporting practices.

After vaguely contemplating the important financial factors, BJ had a revelation accompanied by a sense of deja vu came to light. His mind was racing with the same questions he and Taylor had asked when evaluating their business association. Upon further reflection, he simply concluded many of the financial considerations from one deal to next are fundamentally alike. For him to make a critical evaluation of the most recent proposed business opportunity should be no more than a matter of repeating the mantra for success.

1. Start at Home

- Phase Out Bootstrapping
- Prioritize An Emergency Fund
- Reduce Household Expenses
- Supplement Household Income
- Spend Less, Make More & Save The Difference

Business Income, Wages & Salary
\+ Investment Income
= Diversified Income Streams

90-10 Rule for Spending vs. Savings
\+ Asset Liquidity Management
= Free Cash

Diverse Income Streams
\+ Personal Spending Controls
\+ Strategic Reinvestment of Free Cash
= Keys to Wealth Building

2. Set the Right Course

- Set the Course for Profitable Growth
- Provide Financial Leadership
- Devise a Winning Financial Game Plan
- Aim for a Healthy Bottom Line
- Identify Measures of Success

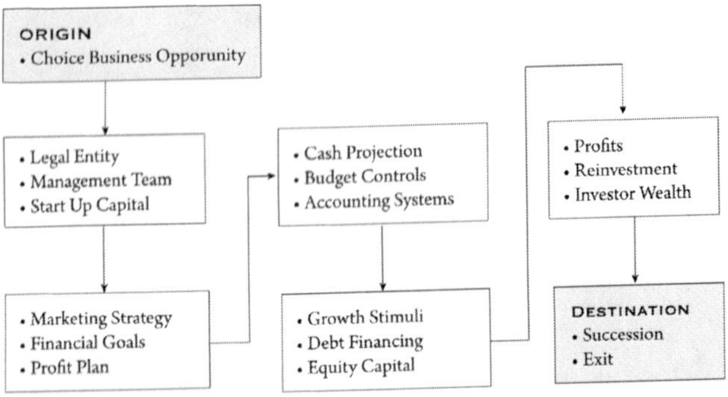

3. Avoid the Classic Pitfalls

- *The Mirage*—Avoid the illusion of profitability
- *Structural Losses*—Deficit pricing and flawed cost estimation causes built-in losses
- *Crippling Growth*—Growth on the back of slow paying accounts depletes cash flow
- *Crisis Culture*—Management solely based on emergency response creates a culture of chaos
- *Lose Oversight*—Financial performance declines in absence of monitoring from the top
- *Complacency*—Over reliance on single product, service or customer can lead to demise
- *Profit Planning*—An intuitive approach is far less reliable than a concrete agenda

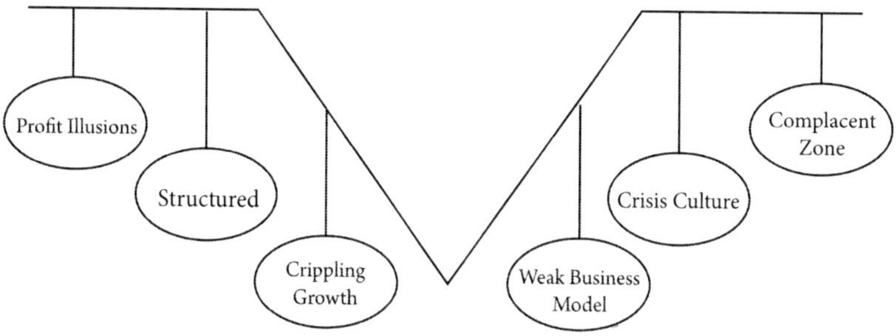

4. Plot a Positive Cash Flow

- Short-term business survival depends on a *positive cash flow*
- Billing, collection, purchases, payroll and operating disbursements should be in sync
- Plot your game plan using a *cash flow projection*
- Improve cash flow through minimizing collection float and maximizing disbursement float

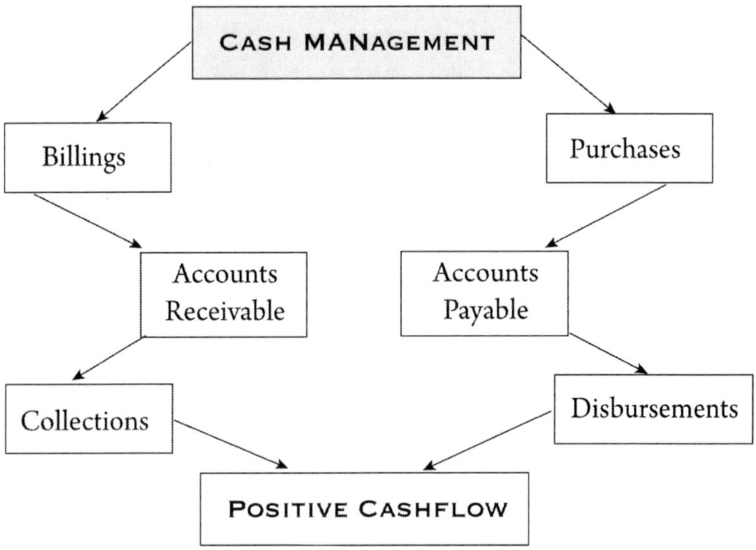

5. "Net" Trumps "Gross"

- Grow the top line and bottom line simultaneously
- Identify breakeven performance where sales revenues cover expenses
- Use profit models to promote "what if" scenario planning
- Higher profit margins on products or services yield more for the bottom line
- Product pricing should be tied to breakeven and profit objectives

PROFIT BUILDING BLOCKS

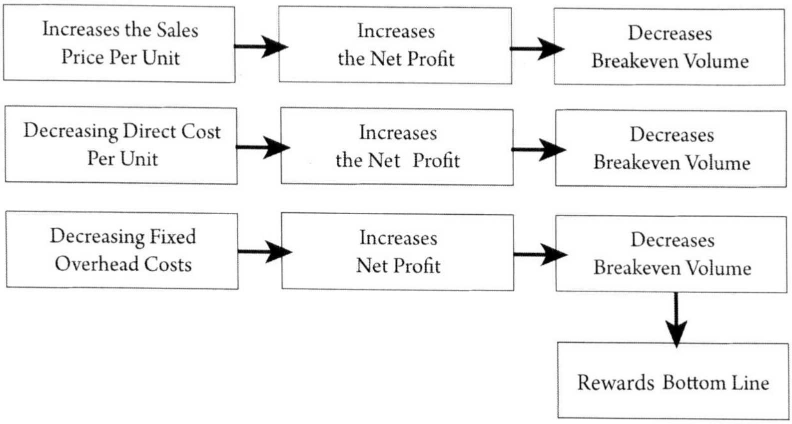

6. Leverage Your Financials

- A *comprehensive set of financial statements* will tell your story for bankers and investors
- *Generally Accepted Accounting Principles* provide universal standards for financial reporting financial information
- Financial vitality is widely measured according to profit & loss, assets and liabilities, and cash flow
- Prospective lenders and investors regard financial statements as a litmus test for further consideration of a financing request

MANAGERIAL USES

Income Statement	Cash Flow Statement	Balance Sheet
Net Earnings Profit Potential Financial Performance	Sources and Uses of Cash	Assets Liabilities Equity

VS

FINANCIER'S USES

Income Statement	Cash Flow Statement	Balance Sheet
Net Earnings Profit Potential Financial Results	Sources and Uses of Cash	Asset Mix Debt Load Owner's Equity

7. Monetize the Enterprise

- Vital indicators tell whether an enterprise is sufficiently monetized
- Industry norms are standards by which good financial health and fitness is measured
- *Efficiency, liquidity and financial return* are key health signs
- Financial ratios and percentages allow for business and industry comparisons
- Internal controls promote compliance with company policies constituting checks and balances
- Audits, reviews and compilations heighten the credibility of your financial statements

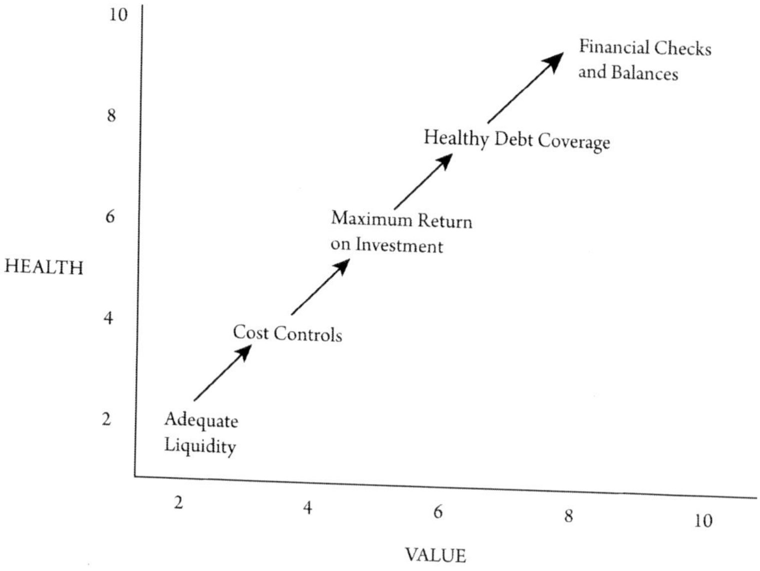

8. Finance Your Dream

- Access to *capital is critical to finance growth* and expansion
- Sources of capital come in two forms, *debt and equity*
- Typical financing needs are driven by business growth, build up in accounts receivables, purchase of business equipment and business acquisitions
- The ideal financing partner should have the strength to meet your current and future funding requirements
- Financing structure should align repayment obligations with expected future income streams and cash flows
- An up to date financing dossier is critical to facilitate a quick response to a financial request

FINANCING ALTERNATIVES

Debt	Equity
Lines of Credit	Owner's Capital
Term Loan	Angel Investors
Asset-Based Receivables Financing	Venture Capital Investors
Mortgage Borrowing	Public Offerings

9. Instill Peak Performance

- Profitability is performance driven
- Financial benchmarks set the stage for peak performance
- Performance measures include *sales, production, profit and return on investment*
- Activity budgets help track work flow to assure profitability
- Financial budgeting is an effective tool used to manage monetary outcomes
- Variance analysis helps identify trouble spots and the underlying causes
- Controlling financial drivers is leadership's responsibility

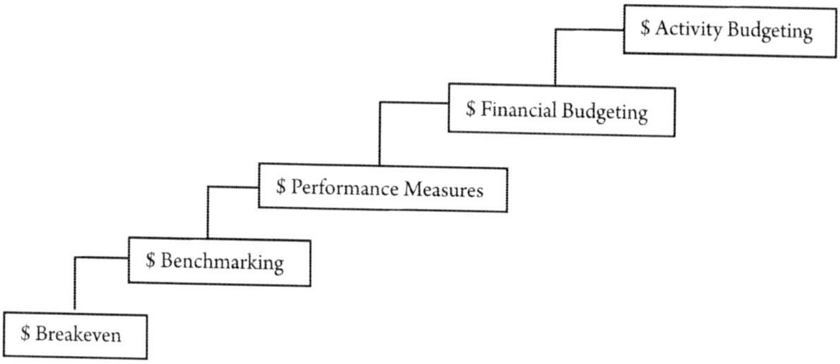

10. Tighten Up Legally

- A solid legal infrastructure provides asset protection
- Limited legal liability protection mitigates risk of personal loss to investors
- A legal business entity is for self-defense in case of business related lawsuits
- Teaming relationships should be embraced by a formal legal document
- Buy-sell agreements specify valuation in the event of a transition of ownership as well as other agreed upon terms of management operation
- Corporate bylaws and LLC operating agreements both outline and tighten the organizational business structure

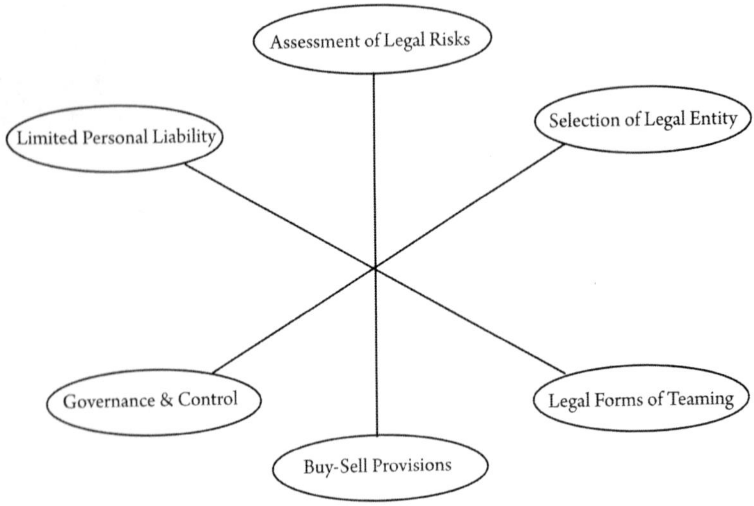

11. Downsize Business Risks

- If you do not *control foreseeable risks*, they will control you
- It pays to actively seek alternatives to offset the worst case scenario
- A *cash reserve* provides capacity for recovery
- Insurance coverage helps soften the financial impact of loss due to death, disability or serious illness
- Boards of advisors and directors help keep leadership fresh and active
- A succession plan provides an exit strategy via business sale, transfer or other type of business disposition

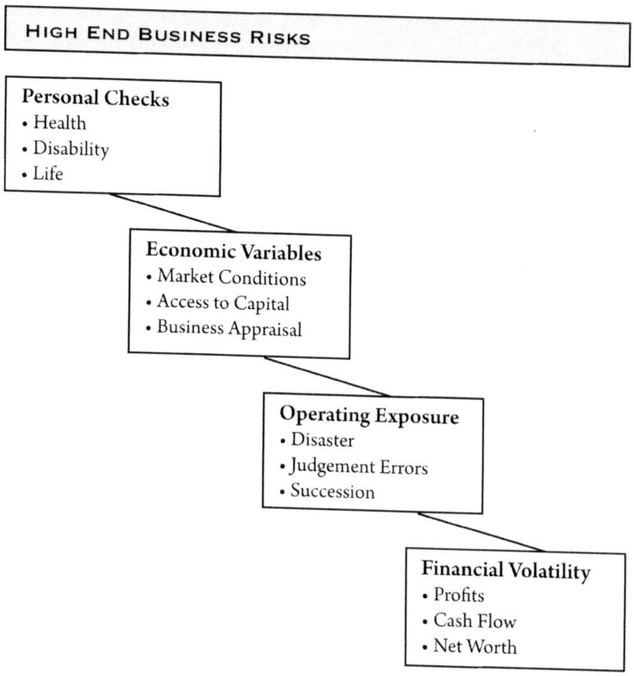

12. Pinpoint Strategic Priorities

- Set forth specific strategic priorities in advance
- Plan to set aside reserves over time
- Work toward building adequate liquidity
- Earnings and profits are not necessarily available for distribution to investors
- Seed money for business reinvestment are necessary to remain competitive
- Income tax reserves are non-discretionary
- Debt management is a leadership responsibility

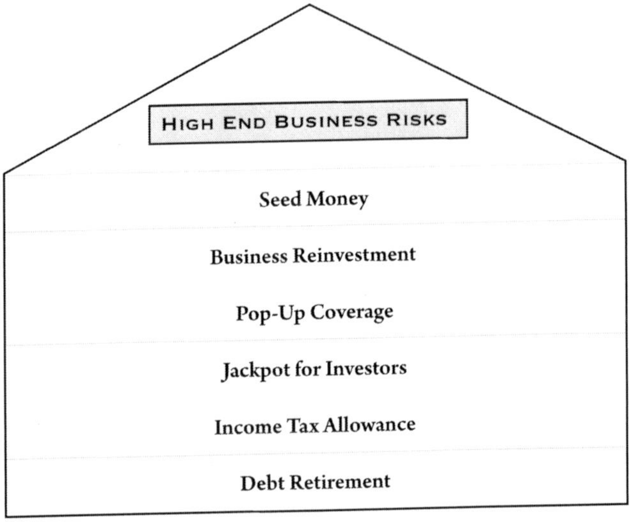

13. Champion Profitable Growth

- Profitable growth achieves balance between *sales, growth, cash flow and profit*
- A strong financial support system is necessary to champion profitable growth
- Unmanaged growth will undermine financial stability
- Sustaining profitable performance over the long-term is the end game
- Finish in the Black

The Road to MegaSuccess

+ Sales Strategies

+ Profit Parameters

+ Cash Flow Support

+ Financing Capacity

+ Internal Control Systems

+ Performance Oversight

+ Risk Management

= Profitable Growth

14. Enriching the Bottom Line

The Mantra

1. Start from Home
2. Set the Right Course
3. Avoid the Classic Pitfalls
4. Plot a Positive Cash Flow
5. "Net" Trumps Gross
6. Leverage Your Financials
7. Monetize the Enterprise
8. Finance the Dream
9. Instill Peak Performance
10. Tighten Up Legally
11. Downsize Business Risks
12. Pinpoint Strategic Priorities
13. Champion Profitable Growth

GLOSSARY

Assets—Includes both tangible and intangible items of value held by the company for future benefit. Generally, most assets held are exchangeable or saleable for some amount of money. For accounting purposes asset values are generally reported at the lower of purchase price or market value.

Audit—Generally, describes the process wherein a CPA examines, on a test basis, evidence supporting the balances, values and disclosures reported in the financial statements. An audit includes assessing the accounting principles used for significant estimates made by management, as well as evaluation of the overall financial statement presentation. Audits provide a reasonable basis for CPAs opinion on whether the financial statements are presented fairly in all material respects.

Budget—A budget is a compilation of financial estimates focusing on expected future sources and uses of funds. A budget should be used as a management tool for overseeing costs of operation and for establishing a plan to maximize available resources. Most organizations and businesses prepare separate budgets for operations versus expenditures for equipment, improvements and other capital expenditures.

Balance Sheet—Addresses liquidity and changes in net worth via reports that detail company assets, liabilities and equity. A balance sheet will pinpoint financial status at the end of a month, quarter or year.

Capital—Refers to funds invested by owners and shareholder to support building and growing a business enterprise. Adequate capita serves to relieve pressure to ramp up sales faster than is reasonable or desirable

Cash Flow Statement—Breakdown of cash activity by listing all sources and uses of cash tied to operations, capital infusions or loans. This report captures cash activity that occurrence during a month, quarter or year.

Compilation—Represents financial information reported on by a CPA. The pertinent data comes in the form of financial statement that is the representation of management (the owners). For purposes of a compilation, CPAs do not audit or review the financial statements and, accordingly, do not express an opinion or any other form of assurance on them.

Crowdfunding—The practice of funding a project or venture by raising many small amounts of money from a large number of people via the internet. Crowdfunding aims to leverage the collective effort of friends, family, customers and individual investors.

Equity—Represent net dollar difference between the stated values of the company assets and liabilities.

Expenses—The costs fully incurred by the business and typically are divided into costs of goods sold (items needed to produce a product or service) and operating expenses (items such as rent, salaries, insurance and advertising incurred in managing the business).

Financial Statements—Generally, this term refers to a balance sheet, income statement and statement of cash flows. The reports are universally recognized as the most comprehensive way to report financial condition, results of operation and cash flow especially when prepared according to Generally Accepted Accounting Principles.

Income Statement—Measures profitability – revenues from sales less costs of products or services and any other expenses necessary to operate the business. Normally covers a month, quarter, or year.

Investment Risk—Risk is any uncertainty your investment value might rise or fall because of market conditions. Investment risk per se describes the probability or likelihood of occurrence of losses relative to the expected return on any particular investment.

Liabilities—Legally enforceable claims and financial obligations for vendor invoices, taxes and outstanding loans.

Liquidity—The availability of liquid assets equivalent to cash for meeting immediate and short term obligations, or assets that can quickly be converted to serve in this manner.

Profit Margin—The difference between the unit selling price of a product or service and direct costs to make the product or render the services.

Revenues—Comprise gross funds received in dollars or amounts billed by a company to its customers for sale of goods and services.

Review—An inspection conducted by a CPA comprised of inquiries of company personnel and analytical procedures applied to financial data. It is substantially less in scope than an audit in accordance with generally accepted auditing standards, the objective of which is the expression of an opinion regarding the financial statements taken as a whole.

Sources of Cash—Include net income, proceeds from bank loans, and contributions by owners as well as sale of assets.

Uses of Cash—Include payment of operating expenses, loan payments, equipment purchases, and real estate purchases investments in other assets.

Volatility—The degree of variation of a trading price over time as measured a standard deviation or pattern. The more spread apart trading prices, the higher the deviation.

ENDNOTES

CHAPTER THREE

Avoid the Classic Pitfalls… Evade the Fault Line

1 United States, Small Business Administration, "Advocacy: The Voice of Small Business in Government 2006 Frequently Asked Questions," June 2006, July 15, 2006 http://www.sba.gov/advo/stats/sbfaq.pdf.

The U.S. Small Business Administration reported the following with regard to business formations and closures:

> Just fewer than 600,000 new businesses with employees are formed each year, and approximately 550,000 firms with employees close each year.
>
> Approximately two-thirds of new employers survive at least two years, however, only one-half make it four years or more.

2 Webb, Allen, "Starbucks' Quest for Healthy Growth: An Interview with Howard Schultz," *McKinsey Quarterly*, March 2011.

3 Lee, Kathlee, "Case Study: Starbucks Coffee," 2010

4 Starbucks Corporation Fiscal 2011 Annual Report

5 Benoit, David, "Tea Time for Starbucks: Coffee Giant to Spend $620 Million on Teavana," *Wall Street Journal*, November 14, 2012.

6 "Eisner Abruptly Shuts Down," *Baltimore Sun*, November 11, 2006.

CHAPTER FOUR
Plot A Positive Cash Flow... Map Distance and Direction

1 "How to Make Money the Buffet Way," *U.S. News and World Report*, August 6, 2007, page 49.

2 Nystedt, Dan, "Dell Eyes $3 Billion in Cost Savings in 3 Years," InfoWorld (www.infoworld.com), April 1, 2008.

3 Dell Inc. Annual Report Fiscal Year 2008.

4 "Dell Delivers Record Results in Fiscal-Year 2011 Fourth Quarter and Full Year," Dell Computers (www.content.dell.com), February 15, 2011.

5 Murray, Eliott, "Dell: A Growth Story In Deep Value Territory," Seeking Alpha (www.seeking alpha.com), October 27, 2012.

CHAPTER FIVE
"Net" Trumps "Gross" ... Adopt the Golden Rule

1 "Seeking Perfect Prices, CEO Tears Up the Rules," *Wall Street Journal*, March 27, 2007.

2 Parker Hannifin Corp., www.parker.com.

CHAPTER SEVEN
Monetize the Enterprise... Build Economic Stamina

1 "Rich are eccentric; All Others Just Crazy," Life Meets Work, www.lifemeetswork.com, March 3, 2010.

2 Wang, Jennifer, "Patagonia, From the Ground Up," Entrepreneur.com, May 12, 2010.

3 Reinhardt, Forest, Casadesus-Masanell, Ramon and Kim, Hyun Jin, "Patagonia," Harvard Business School Publishing, Boston, Massachusetts, 2010.

4 Chouinard, Yvon, Let My People Go Surfing: The Education of a Reluctant Businessman, Penguin Books, 2006.

CHAPTER EIGHT
Finance the Dream... Accelerate the Breakthrough

1. Google Corporate Milestones, January 2006, http://www.google.com/intl/en/corporate/history.html, March 15, 2006.
2. MMG Financial Funds, Meridian Management Group, Inc., http://www.mmggroup.com, December 2012.

CHAPTER NINE
Instill Peak Performance... Inspect What You Expect

1. Thompson, Derek, "Zara's Big Idea: What the World's Top Fashion Retailer Tells Us About Innovation," *The Atlantic Magazine*, November 13, 2012.
2. Dishman, Linda, "The Strategic Retail Genius Behind Zara," *Forbes* online, March 23, 2012.
3. Inditex Corporation 2011 Annual Report.
4. Damodaran, Aswath, Margins by Sector, NYU Leonard Stern School of Business, January 2012.
5. "Zara Case Study: Fast Fashion from Savvy Systems," Flat World Knowledge, Inc., www.flatworldknowledge.come/node/19554.
6. Cuadros, Alex, "Bad News is Good News for Clothier Zara," *The Washington Post*, November 10, 2012.
7. Perez de Pablos, Susana, "The Reluctant Entrepreneurs," *El Pais*, September 24, 2012.
8. Mlot, Stephanie, "Apple Stores Top Tiffany's in Retail Sales Per Square Foot," PCMAG.COM, http://www.pcmag.com/article2/0,2817,2412094,00.asp, November 12, 2012.
9. Scott Martin, "How Apple Beat Tiffany," *Red Herring*, http://www.redherring.com/Article.aspx?a=200332&hed=How+Appl..., July 24, 2007.
10. Jena McGregor, "Leading Listener: Trader Joe's," *Fast Company*.com, http://www.fastcompany.com/magazine/87/customer-traderjoes.htm, October 2004.

11 Eric Monnoyer and Stefan Spang, "Manufacturing Lessons for Service Industries: An Interview with AXA;s Claude Brunet," *McKinsey Quarterly* (Spring 2005), 11.

12 Monnoyer and Spang, "Manufacturing Lessons for Service Industries," 12.

13 *Supply Chain Security Best Practices Catalog, Customs-Trade Partnership Against Terrorism*, U.S. Customs and Borer Protection, January 2006, iii.

CHAPTER TWELVE

Pinpoint Strategic Priorities... Stockpile Reserves

1 Behind Microsoft's Bid to Gain Cutting Edge," *Wall Street Journal*, July 30, 2007.

2 "Microsoft's Curse: An Uninspired CEO or Its Own Lifecycle?" *The Washington Post*, September 6, 2013.

3 "Looking Forward: S&T for the 21st Century," National Research Council Canada, http://www.nrc-cnrc.gc.ca/aboutUs/ren/nrc-foreshight_10_e.html, September 16, 2005.

4 "Economy Slows But May Hold Seeds of Growth," *Wall Street Journal*, April 28, 2007.

5 World Population Prospects: The 2006 Revision," *Fact Sheet, Series A*, United Nations Department of Economic and Social Affairs, Population Division, Population Estimates and Projections Section, March 2007.

CHAPTER THIRTEEN

Champion Profitable Growth... Finish in the Black

1 Jason Dedrick, Kenneth L. Kraemer and Bryan MacQuarrie, "Gateway Computer: Using E-Commerce to Move 'Beyond the Box' and to Move More Boxes," Center for Research on information Technology and Organizations, University of California, Irvine, February 2001, and Susan Kichinskas, "Gateway Stores Put Out to Pasture," *Internetnews.com*, http://www.internetnews.com/bus-news/print.php/3334901, April 2, 2004.

[2] "Burned by Last Boom, Boeing Curbs Its Pace," *Wall Street Journal*, March 26, 2007.

[3] Jeremy Cato, "Toyota's Global Strategy Looks Inward," in ToyotaNation.com, http://www.toyotanation.com/forum/showthread.php?1=54954, October 28, 2004.

[4] Allan Cohen, James Watkinson and Jenny Boone, "Herb Kelleher Talks about How Southwest Airlines Grew from Entrepreneurial Startup to Industry Leadership," Babson Insight, http://www.babsoninsight.com/contentmgr/showdetails.php/id/829, Babson University.

Louis G. Hutt, Jr., Esq., C.P.A.

Louis G. Hutt, Jr. is a native of St. Louis, Missouri. He graduated from Washington University with a Bachelor of Science in Business Administration and joined the audit staff of Ernst and Young Certified Public Accountants. While with Ernst and Young, Hutt was selected to serve as the firm's Visiting Professor of Accounting at Morgan State University.

Upon completing his executive teaching assignment, Hutt attended the University of Maryland School of Law. While there, he interned with the Securities Division of the Maryland Attorney General's Office and clerked for the Honorable Chief Judge Robert Bell who is now Chief Judge of the Maryland Court of Appeals. After completing law school, Hutt established The Law Office of Louis G. Hutt, Jr. and Bennett, Hutt and Co., L.L.C., Certified Public Accountants.

His law practice focuses on representation in tax controversies, contract negotiation, business acquisitions, and business law planning involving the formation of legal entities including tax exempt organizations. Bennett, Hutt and Co., provides executive level management training as well as business, tax and management advisory services to an array of entrepreneurs, professional offices, professional sports, and different regulated organizations. Offices are maintained in Columbia, Maryland and Albuquerque, New Mexico.

Hutt is a weekly guest on XM 169 morning radio talk show (The Madison Show) from Washington D.C. He has been recognized as the Distinguished Alumni of the School of Business by Washington University; U.S. Small Business Administration as Accounting Advocate of the Year; Waring-Mitchell Law Society's Distinguished Member of the Community Award; Practitioner of the Year by University of Maryland's Black Law Students Association; recipient of NAACP Business Award; and Alpha Kappa Alpha Sorority's Meritorious Service Award.

Louis is also a proud member of Alpha Phi Alpha Fraternity, Inc.

280721-250-10-60W